Mainly by Bike

A SENIOR CYCLIST TOURS THE WORLD

ANN WILSON

Published in 2017 by Ann Wilson

ISBN: 978-1-9998936-0-6
Book & Cover Design by Russell Holden

www.pixeltweakspublications.com

Illustrations by Pete Langley

Printed by Ingram

For my children
Matthew and Vanessa

Foreword

With all the interest in cycling and the need to exercise more at the moment, this is an excellent 'put your money where your mouth is' story. It is written by someone, who at the age of 59, and a late convert to cycling, proved that at any age you can really enjoy riding a bike, albeit a bit of an extreme adventure if you had only limited experience of cycle touring.

This isn't a dull travel log, it moves along nicely – most days the miles that are covered by bike are just mentioned in passing. As well as meeting 'interesting' people along the way there's the 'excitement' of finding lodgings for the night, not an easy thing to do if you are on your own, in a foreign country and it's late at night and raining.

After a sedate start travelling through the nicer parts of Europe (when the saddle soreness kicks in) the journey is followed by the excitement of India and not-so-nice experiences early on in Asia then the long ride through North America. Ann proves that if you really want to experience countries to their fullest, do it on your own, and the number of new friends she meets and stays with along the way proves this point.

Apart from Ann being the 'star' of the book, credit must be given to the bike(s) (one was stolen – now I know why riders take their bike into their room). The second bike was an eastern European type, not noted for lightness but it still proved its worth. These bikes underwent so much ... ridden daily, put in sheds, packed in boxes, boarded on trains, planes, buses, and various cars and used again & again. They were loaded with panniers front and back, and got Ann safely around the world and back home to Ulverston.

This is a must-read book for anyone who dreams of adventure but just needs a nudge in the right direction to get up and do it.

Paul Loftus MBE
President of The Fred Whitton Challenge

Preface

In the summer of 2007, I was walking with the Ramblers in the Lakeland fells and mentioned to a friend that I'd once cycled from Carlisle to Ipswich. Sometime later, she gave me a book called *'A Bike Ride'* by Anne Mustoe, little knowing the chain of events she was sparking. I found the story so inspiring that within a year I'd made up my mind: I would quit my job, let my spare room to pay the bills, and make a similar journey cycling around the world. I was approaching sixty, and life was suddenly too short to delay this mission any longer than necessary.

Over the next twelve months I spent many hours researching equipment, studying maps, reading online journals and devouring as many cycling books as I could – more Anne Mustoe, Dervla Murphy and Alastair Humphreys, to name a few. As the departure date approached, I did a test ride from Berwick-on-Tweed to Penrith, and rode a few circuits of Coniston Water to remind myself just what life on the road was like. I was a long way from being 'bike-fit', but I could manage thirty miles a day, and expected to raise that to fifty-plus as my fitness level improved en route. However, there would be no pressure and no one to compete with, so I could go at my own pace. … and there I was two years later, just turned fifty-nine, taking early retirement at the end of June, and about to begin the biggest adventure of my life. "You're very brave", people kept saying, – and I hadn't even set off. I knew I had to earn that kind of praise before I could agree. But funnily enough, no one called me mad. That went without saying.

Contents

Part One

Part Two

Part Three

Bulgaria – August 2009

In the morning, I packed my bags and carried them down to the bottom floor to load up my bike. It seems almost dreamlike now, as I remember reaching the basement and seeing that the padlock was missing. With some effort, I pulled on the heavy iron door and strained my eyes against the darkness, anxiously fumbling around the wall to find the light switch. In the inky blackness the switch eluded me and I tentatively reached out to feel for my bike. My heart sank and a cold numbness crept over my body as my hand fell through the air. I groped among the dust and cobwebs and this time found the switch. In the gloomy yellow light, all I could see was an empty space where my beautiful bike should be. 'I'm not thinking clearly', I told myself, 'there's bound to be an explanation', and with a knot in my stomach I climbed the stone steps of the peeling, echoing stairwell to speak to my hosts. I knocked on their apartment door and Ivo answered. "There's probably a good reason for this," I said, "but my bike's not in the basement". One look at his puzzled face told me that my worst fears were about to be confirmed. We ran down what now seemed like endless flights of steps to the ground floor. Ivo entered the basement and climbed over the dusty trestles and old broken furniture, searching the recesses of the room. With a perplexed expression, he walked outside and looked around the unkempt grassy area, one hand on the back of his head, his total bewilderment becoming ever more apparent. No doubt about it – the bike had gone.

Part I

A Steep Learning Curve

"I want to do it!"

"If you want to do it – DO it!" This was my daughter's response as I constantly updated her on my heroine's exploits while reading *'A Bike Ride'*. My utterances were becoming monotonous. "But how can I give up a good job and still pay a mortgage?" I asked. "If you *want* to do it, you'll find a way," she said. And so my daughter gave me the wisest advice I could have heard.

It was summer 2008 and I was fifty-eight. I'd reached senior management level with my company and I was living well within my means. I had savings – for what? – a rainy day? – retirement? The cogs were going round in my head – perhaps I could let the house while I was away or maybe rent out the rooms and leave my daughter in charge? Did I want to make this trip *that* much? Yes, – I did. The seed was sown.

The announcement that I was going to cycle around the world was received with amusement and a certain amount of disbelief by my two brothers, but as the weeks wore on and I continued to show them newly acquired pieces of camping equipment, it began to sink in that this was no fantasy – I was serious.

My first purchase was a cheap one-man tent, which I erected on brother Mike's lawn. With so little camping experience, I needed to imagine how it would feel to spend night after night in that tiny space. I crawled in and looked around. I could do this.

The next twelve months of preparation involved hours of research on the internet, reading books and online journals, studying maps and visa requirements, and visiting bike and camping shops. My daughter had agreed to look after the house in my absence, so, at the same time, I was busy decorating tired-looking bedrooms for the new occupants. The first tent was swapped for something more robust, and I equipped myself with everything I needed to take me on a twelve-to-fifteen-month journey. The total weight came to twenty-two kilos and that was without food or liquids. My panniers would have to be strong and waterproof and I opted for those made by Ortlieb, which I knew many cycle tourists used – two on the front, two at the back and a roomy bar-bag. Choosing a bike was probably the most difficult decision. After much consideration, I bought the best I could afford – a hand-built Roberts Roughstuff with a Rohloff hub – the 'Rolls Royce' of gear systems. It was expensive, but I reasoned that at my age, it would last me the rest of my cycling life.

I decided to take a small netbook with me and to keep an online journal on the *'crazyguyonabike'* website, a popular resource for touring cyclists. The site was packed with useful information for a trip like mine and had been a vital tool for my research. It was free to use and seemed like the ideal way to keep family and friends updated, without dropping lengthy round-robins into their mailboxes, which they may feel obliged to read.

The netbook was fitted with a camera, so I would also be able to use it to talk to family through Skype. I would just need a wifi connection, which I expected to frequently have. In 2009 smartphones were not as ubiquitous as they are now and I didn't have one. The word 'selfie' was yet to be coined and selfie-sticks hadn't been invented. Handheld mapping technology was expensive, so I would have to rely on what paper maps I could find.

As for me, I was in pretty poor shape. Working from home has many advantages but being within easy reach of a well-stocked fridge is an unfortunate one. My life had been sedentary for too long – when I wasn't sat at a desk answering emails or in conference calls, I was spending hours driving down the motorway to attend meetings.

Training was relatively minimal. In August 2008 I made a 4-day test trip from Berwick-on-Tweed to Penrith, to see if I could still ride a loaded bike. This was a great success, but a long harsh winter followed, giving me little encouragement to leave the house again. Over the coming months, my weight soared to almost 160lbs (not good when you're five foot three and a half.) Nevertheless, I considered myself much fitter than I deserved to be, and still managed weekly walks to the tops of the Lakeland fells and the odd thirty-mile ride round Coniston Water.

In January 2009, I took the final step and applied for early retirement. This was the last piece of the jigsaw and it would be May before my release came through. By mid-June I was able to fix my leaving date.

My route was fairly well-defined as far as Turkey, but anything beyond was fluid, mainly because I wasn't sure I would even make it that far. Many countries tantalised me. I was keen to visit Iran, I knew I wanted to see India and South East Asia, and if I made it as far as Singapore I would reassess. North America seemed too huge to comprehend, so it didn't seem worth investing too much time worrying about at this stage. Maybe I'd have had enough by then – maybe I would fly home and finish the American leg later – maybe, maybe, maybe.... I had no idea how I would cope on my own for so long, and it therefore seemed foolish to make too many detailed plans. This view was endorsed shortly before I left, when I came across a quote from Alastair Humphreys in his book, *'Ten Lessons from the Road'* – "Think like a goldfish", he said. What a wonderful maxim. Have a rough idea about what lies ahead, but only worry about the immediate. I left with one map of northern France in my panniers.

GB

Departure

On July 11th, my daughter and I drove to Boroughbridge in North Yorkshire, where I would spend the night before catching the Bike Express coach to Calais the next morning. The situation seemed surreal. Was I really doing this? We unloaded the bike and panniers, hugged and said our slightly awkward farewells, knowing it would be at least a year before the next hug. When I settled down for the night, I found a small card slipped into my bar bag. On it was written –

I love you every mile of the way
Your year, your adventure
Be the best you've ever been!
Love, your very proud daughter
Vanessa xxx

The coach turned out to be not as express as it claimed. It broke down twice near Sheffield, resulting in a very late arrival on the outskirts of Calais at dusk. I disembarked with two other passengers in a layby beside a deserted wasteland, and the coach drove off into the night. The other cyclists had reserved a pitch at a nearby campsite, and with hindsight I should have followed them, instead of which, my lack of experience sent me hunting for a 'chambre d'hôte' (B&B) in the nearby town of Ardres. By the time I found 'Le Fuchsia', it was half past ten and dark. A single light was on in the kitchen and I tentatively knocked at the front door. Hope faded fast when the proprietors told me they were full, but despair turned to relief when they made a call and found me a room in a nearby hotel. Up the road I pedalled, to a gloomy old place with narrow stairs and dark flowery wallpaper. Notwithstanding the décor, it had been a long day and the room was a welcome resting place. I had a good night's sleep and looked forward to getting down to the task ahead the next morning.

U.K.
LONDON
NETHERLANDS
BERLIN
WARSAW
POLAND
CALAIS
BELGIUM
COLOGNE
GERMANY
PRAGUE
CZECHIA
UKRAINE
PARIS
MUNICH
SLOVAKIA
BESANÇON
AUSTRIA
BUDAPEST
MOLDOVA
FRANCE
SWITZERLAND
HUNGARY
ROMANIA
SLOVENIA
ZAGREB
VENICE
MILAN
CROATIA
SERBIA
BOSNIA AND HERZEGOVINA
BUCHAREST
MONACO
SARAJEVO
SOFIA
ITALY
MONTE NEGRO
KOSOVO
BULGARIA
ANDORRA
ROME
ALBANIA
ISTANBUL
MACEDONIA
PAIN
BARCELONA
BURSA
VALENCIA
GREECE
ATHENS
TURKEY

France

Early mistakes

After a late breakfast, I left Ardres in a buoyant mood and cycled to St Omer, where I parked myself on a bench outside the cathedral and took out my lunch. Today it was dried sausage with tomatoes and French bread, followed by banana and cake. It all seemed very civilised and indeed it was. I wasn't to know how my standards would slip in the coming months, but right now it was one of my many 'This is the life!' moments. The sun was shining, the cathedral was a picture, and I was on my way.

Despite my enthusiasm, I knew I had a lot to learn and I wasn't naïve enough to expect things to be easy at the start. My inauspicious arrival hadn't been perfect, and on the second day I rode for twelve hours before I was able to lay my head down for the night. There were a number of reasons for this: one – I was lost for much of the time, two – the north of France is very flat, and three – I couldn't find anywhere to sleep.

Looking back, it seems that everything I did could have been done better, and so it could. For the beginner cycling tourist, every task takes longer than it does for the experienced. Packing panniers, clipping them on the racks, deciding what to keep handy at the top and what to carry in your bar-bag, deciding what clothes to wear, what food to buy, and very importantly, when to ask for help. At the start, it was probably this last task which I found the hardest.

Cycling into St Omer had been straightforward, but getting out was far from easy. Every road I followed led me to the motorway and it was only by chance that I finally hit upon the road to Lillers. Finding my way into the centre of Lillers was another struggle and various wrong turns added on more miles than were necessary. It was 5.30pm before I finally sailed in on the main street. My hopes were set on camping, and as luck would have it, there was a campsite on the edge of town. It was at this point that I made my first big mistake. I now know that when you arrive at a campsite after the office has closed, what you do is march through the gateway and pitch your tent, in the sure knowledge that the owners will almost definitely find you in the morning and ask for the fee. What did I do? – I turned away. I can only think that the stress of the moment had addled my brain and knocked all common sense out of it.

Feeling more than a little fraught, I set off to look for a B&B. I must have ridden every feeder road in and out of Lillers, covering another mile each time and finding zilch. It was becoming highly likely that I'd be spending the night in a hotel, and at this rate, I'd blow my budget before I'd crossed Europe.

On the way out the town, some movement on the tarmac ahead caught my eye and I saw a family of stoats trying to cross the busy road. With their chocolate bodies and creamy breasts, they are among the most beautiful of wild creatures. They were five very young stoats and by the time I reached them, two had been hit and the remaining three were in a state of panic, running in all directions. There was no sign of the parents and further carnage was inevitable. I couldn't bear to see the final outcome and pedalled on.

By evening, I was running out of daylight and my legs were running out of power. There were no guest houses or indeed hotels, so wild camping was now becoming my only choice. I scanned the fields as I rode, but the vast grain monoculture of northern France offered little cover for a surreptitiously placed tent. All the uncultivated areas were enclosed and it was almost dark when I finally found an unfenced wood and wandered up a track until I was out of sight from the road. Feeling like a convict on the run, I hid my bike in the bushes and skipped pegging the tent so that I could make a quick getaway. I set my alarm for 6am and crawled into my sleeping bag. It wasn't the best night's sleep but at least I was under cover. I was fully packed and away by 6.45 the next morning.

It was time to reassess. I had expected to find more accommodation options and had read that many French towns and villages pride themselves on their campsites. Up to now, I wasn't finding this to be the case. B&Bs were scarce and campsites were poorly signed. With hindsight, I can see that my choice of route had something to do with this, and I needed to buy a campsite directory, but this came with its own problems. I'd arrived on a Saturday at the start of a Bank Holiday weekend (Bastille Day to be precise) – three days when the main shops were closed. Monday night I was back in a hotel and on Tuesday, Bastille Day, I was again hopelessly failing to find somewhere to stay. I'd seen a few guest houses in the morning but none when I needed them. This was some introduction to being a world traveller.

By 7pm I was tired and hungry and the smell of a pizza van in the village of Epehy made me decide I'd be much better off with some food inside me. Behind the counter, Gilles the owner asked me how I was. In my best French (which isn't that good), I said, "I'm tired, I can't find a chambre d'hôte or a campsite and I'll be sleeping in the woods". "Au contraire mon ami!" – he didn't actually say that, what he did say was that there was a campsite six kilometres away in Honnecourt.

In the morning, I packed up my tent, and after a breakfast of leftover pizza, headed for the shops.

On the way to St Quentin, I passed through the small, appropriately named town of Fins (fin is French for end), and stopped at the cemetery to look at the war graves. The acres of white head stones stretched out in front of me and as I stepped on the grass, my eyes welled. Reading the inscriptions on the stones was heartbreaking. *'Raised to a higher service'*, said one, and another that touched me deeply as a mother, read, *'I know I will one day see the face I have loved again. Mum.'* It moves me even now as I write.

In St Quentin I bought a camping directory, after which, finding places to stay was plain sailing (or should that be plain cycling?). I plotted my route via campsites and quickly became an expert at erecting and packing my tent. The weather smiled on me and remained fine in the daytime, though I spent many a night snuggled up in my sleeping bag listening to thunderstorms rattling above me.

Keeping my panniers stocked with food was something of a challenge. Villages in the north of France are very pretty but because most of the land has been turned over to intensive farming on a grand scale, there are no jobs for the young. I was told later that the north west region is referred to as the 'dead zone' by some. Many properties lie empty, and consequently, village shops are few and far between. After a morning of passing through one village after another with nowhere to buy bread, I saw a man coming through the gate of a house carrying a basket with a tea towel over it. 'This looks promising,' I thought, seeing a sign which read 'Boucher et Charcuterie', but I soon did an about-turn when three snarling dogs snapped at me from behind the gate. This might be the village shop, but I was in danger of losing a leg! Summoning up my best school French again, I said to the man, "I am frightened of the dogs. Are they dangerous?" "Not if you stay outside the gate," he said. "They are if you go inside." 'Thanks for that', I thought. 'Very helpful'. A woman followed him out of the house and explained that it was no longer a shop and the nearest bakery was three kilometres away. I now had a race on to get there before noon when no doubt the shop would close until 3pm. I arrived just in time and bought bread, a triple pack of pâté and a tin of sardines. I guessed I'd soon be sick of pâté.

As the days wore on and I headed further south, the weather became warmer, and it was increasingly difficult to keep perishable food for any length of time. Tinned sardines became a daily staple and the oil became a perfectly acceptable substitute for butter or olive oil. It was all part of life on the road.

On the Chemin des Dames plateau, named after the daughters of Louis XV, I stopped at an information board detailing the history of three WWI battles which took place in the surrounding countryside. The peaceful rolling hills belied their bloody past. I was considering the contradiction of the panorama before me and was suddenly struck with an awareness of my presence in the scene. It seemed impossible that I'd reached this far. I looked to the south-east and a voice in my head was telling me 'Italy is over there, and Turkey, and all the countries I'm travelling to' – it was hard to take in. At the bottom of the hill, a field of cheery sunflowers turned to face the road like hundreds of curious smiling faces. Life was good, and in a moment of mad exhilaration, I waved to them from my bike.

In Reims I spent an afternoon wandering round the cathedral and found my way to the 'Cliques and Croques' internet café, to update my journal and talk to my family over Skype. I couldn't yet use my netbook because the one thing I'd forgotten to pack was a European adaptor – something of a problem but not insurmountable. My daughter had put one in the post and I would collect it in St Dizier using the Poste Restante service.

A few days later I picked up the adaptor and found a hotel. It had only taken me a few hours to get to St Dizier, and by 1.30 I was checked in and finally using 'weefee' on my netbook. By three o'clock my bathroom was festooned with washed clothes and my tent was hung out to dry. Feeling altogether happy with life, I cycled into town where I had an enjoyable meal, a few glasses of wine and wobbled back to my room. Things were looking up.

From St Dizier I followed the towpath along the Canal Marne-Saône which would take me all the way to Langres with plenty of campsites along the way. What a pleasure it was to leave the traffic behind for the solitude of the canal. As I cycled along in the sunshine, watching barges negotiate the locks, dragonflies and butterflies escorted me, startled herons took to the air and swallows swooped over the mirror-like surface of the water. There were no exhausting uphills and no exhilarating downhills, just a steady turn, turn, turn of the pedals. I saw few cyclists or pedestrians, and after 100 miles and three relaxing days of enjoying the solitude, I was ready to re-join the traffic.

According to the guidebooks, Langres is one of the fifty most beautiful cities in France. It is steeped in history from the third century AD, and is the birthplace of the philosopher Diderot whose statue stands in the central square. It sits high on a limestone promontory, making it visible from the canal, and, as there was no way I could pedal up the precipitous incline leading to the old town, I pushed. The views from the city walls were stunning and I spent the next day walking their length, and exploring the narrow streets which wind up and down the hillside.

In spite of having cycled more than 600 miles, my quads continued to ache. I had hoped they'd be less painful by now and began to think I wouldn't be truly 'bike-fit' until they stopped screaming at me. I also knew that things were about to become tougher when I reached the Jura Mountains. How would I get over the Swiss Alps I wondered?

The break in Langres did me good and I was ready to stop meandering around the isolated minor lanes and go for the more direct roads. I zoomed out of Langres on a fabulous downhill which seemed to go on forever, and prepared to tackle the now much more hilly terrain and busy major highways – quite a shock after miles of canal towpath.

I camped in the town of Gray and enjoyed the change in climate that heading south brought with it. A laidback Mediterranean quality was in the air and the towns were less neat. There were more people going about their daily life than I ever saw in the north. Cows grazed in meadows bordered by an abundance of forestry, unlike the acres and acres of barley of the north.

Besançon had been a milestone for me while I was scouring the maps over the last 12 months. I always felt I would have broken the back of my first country if I made it this far, and it would be the beginning of the end of France and time to start thinking about Switzerland. This crazy idea was becoming a reality and who knows – maybe it was 'do-able'.

Riding into the city had been fine up to the last five miles or so, and then it was hectic. I dropped off the main road a little too quickly and ended up joining all the commercial traffic. After a lot of unnecessary searching, I found the badly-signed Office de Tourism and asked about hostels. Tourist information offices exist in most large towns around the world, and were usually my first thought when I needed advice, accommodation or maps. They are mostly very helpful, and here the assistant found me a room in an excellent Auberge de Jeunesse, just twenty-four euros for the night, including breakfast.

Next morning, having been advised to avoid the main road out of the city, I joined a cycle path beside the river from where the magnificent fortified city walls were easily visible. Things were going well until I realised I'd gone too far and stopped to look at the map. It wasn't long before a rather dishy cyclist (of a similar age) pulled up and offered to help. He was most impressed with my mileage and my big plan and his suggestion was to get onto the road to Morre. "It's not too steep," he said – (I should have known better, looking at how athletic he was), "and you can take the little road over the main road to La Vese".

Following his advice, I back-tracked a mile or so and found the turning. Regret soon set in as I followed a busy, winding road which snaked up the side of a steep hillside, forcing me to walk on the left along a narrow, paved footpath, facing continuous oncoming traffic. Things were about to get worse when, to my horror, the footpath disappeared behind a crash barrier and became an even narrower track running alongside the road and falling away on my left to the river below. The track was now so narrow I could barely get my panniers past the barrier posts, but I'd reached the point of no return and there was no going back. Nor could I get back on the road beside me without removing the panniers and stopping the traffic so that I could lift the bike over the barrier and then reload it. Having to struggle through the brambles and nettles in my shorts wasn't helping, so I decided to change into my long trousers. With vehicles flying past in both directions, I whipped off my cotton shorts and slipped into my leggings. In spite of the fact that I had cycling shorts on underneath, it must have been somewhat of a distraction to the drivers, and I had to see some comedy in the situation. Finally, after a couple of hair-raising moments, when I slipped and had to grab the barrier to stop myself disappearing down the precipitous banking, a gap appeared in the barrier and the road levelled out. I waited for a break in the traffic and crossed.

The rest of the day was comparatively uneventful, and, in another thirty miles I was in the pretty town of Ornans, where everything for the outdoor pursuits enthusiast can be found, together with plenty of accommodation. At the central campsite, the young male receptionist was very pleasant when he greeted me.

"Yes Madame, we have a place and there is free swimming included and here is a ticket" he said. "It will be twenty-nine euros."

"Twenty-nine euros! But I paid twenty-four euros for a bed in a hostel in Besançon last night! (I forgot to mention the breakfast, en-suite and free wifi.) No! Twelve euros at the most – I have only a tiny tent and a bicycle. I started to leave and there was some muttering between the staff behind the counter.

"Madame – perhaps we can do fifteen euros." I accepted graciously and went off to pitch my tent.

I was cold that night and slept fitfully. At 7am, I woke to a heavy dew and clouds hanging in the valley; it was quite beautiful to watch the swirling mist surrounding the campsite. The inside of my flysheet was covered in condensation and I snuggled back down to wait for the sun to appear and dry it out.

At 11am, I was back on the road and followed cycle paths for five miles on fairly flat going. Around midday, the road started to climb up the side of an impressive gorge slicing through the mountainous Jura. A high limestone escarpment flanked my left and the source de la Loue River disappeared down a deep ravine on my right. Very soon, I ran out of pedal power and started to push. By midday, I was beginning to expire with the heat, and remembering how Dervla Murphy coped in these temperatures in her book 'Full Tilt', I rolled down a track and into a field, where I found a quiet spot and inflated my mattress for a nap.

I woke refreshed and carried on through Ouhans Goux-les-Usiers and Bians-les-Usiers, but the sun was still high, and, by the time I arrived at Sambacour I was exhausted and sweltering. My fluid supply was so low that I'd begun to ration my intake and when I came across a man hosing the forecourt outside his house, I asked, "Could I have some water?" "Non-potable", he said shaking his head. He took my bottles and filled them inside the house and asked where I'd cycled from. "Felicitations (congratulations)" he said when I told him.

There was still more climbing to do, but I was eventually rewarded with two-miles of downhill before the road levelled out and I rolled into Pontarlier. The town sits on an expansive plateau, a feature of the geology of the area, which is ravaged by shifting faults and covered in glacial moraine. After travelling through jagged, mountainous terrain, it was a surprise to arrive at such a wide area of flat land. In the centre, I came to a street market. I walked towards the brightly-hung stalls, where a tall, handsome Swiss cyclist stood with his hand outstretched to greet me – a lovely welcome to the town. He asked about my journey and told me he was touring with his wife and six-month old baby. We walked together through the market until he found his wife who was pulling the child in a trailer. We chatted for some time about cycling in Switzerland and then raised our hands in a 'high-five' and parted. I was beginning to feel part of the cycling community as I wheeled off to find the Auberge de Jeunesse.

Sunday was dull and drizzly, but my luck was still holding as far as the weather went and I still hadn't had a wet cycling day. The rain seemed to only fall at night and on my days off, and today was the day for planning my route through Switzerland. In the hostel I slept well but woke early. Breakfast was poor – bread, jam, cornflakes, milk and cold coffee. I was glad I had my own supplies to supplement the meagre fare.

I went out amongst the umbrellas to find advice on a route out of town, but this time my visit to the tourist information wasn't very productive. There were no useful maps of Switzerland, and the only guidance the assistant could give me was not to take the main road to Lausanne. "It is too dangerous for cyclists," she said. I found a map at a newsagent and reconsidered her advice. Over the following months I would learn that people who don't themselves cycle, would generally tend towards being over-cautious. Only experience tells you how big a pinch of salt to take with such advice and even then, you don't always get it right.

I'd booked dinner at the hostel in advance, and after the disappointing breakfast, my expectations weren't high. That evening, I sat with a dozen others and in fact the meal was very good. The table settings were typically French, with one plate and one set of cutlery to be used throughout the meal for starter, main course and cheese and biscuits. The first three courses were followed by a delicious 'tarte au tatin' which we ate with no plate. On finishing dessert, one of my fellow diners asked me in English where I was going next. Until then, everyone had conversed in French, and with my limitations, I was reluctant to join in. No one had spoken to me except for a nodded 'Bonjour'. When I said I had cycled from Calais and was on my way through Switzerland to Italy, everyone became interested and it turned out that most of them spoke English to a greater or lesser degree. I still felt as if I was regarded as a bit of an oddity, maybe because I was a woman travelling on my own – I don't know.

The next morning, I avoided breakfast and instead grabbed some bread to eat on the way. Two of the Frenchmen saw me loading the bike and queried the weight – "Ten kilos?" they asked. "Twenty-two", I said. They looked suitably impressed.

Switzerland

A wrong turn

I took the main road out of Pontarlier with the intention of diverting onto the secondary road, to reach the Swiss border via Yverdon les Bains. The advice from the tourist information assistant was ringing in my ears, but I found the main road perfectly cycleable and stayed with it to Vallorbe. The scenery was changing once more and I was looking forward to entering my second country. Forests lined the road and covered the steep hillsides; farmers were cutting grass and the fragrance of lavender hung in the air. From the hillside town of Joune, I could see Switzerland in the far distance, and one last swoop took me down to the border checkpoint, where I waved my passport and carried on.

In Lausanne, I strolled round the town centre and bumped into an American who was eager to talk. He was coming to the end of a cycling holiday and lugged a cumbersome cardboard bike box under his arm in readiness for his flight back to Los Angeles. I followed his directions to the tourist information office in the train station so that I could ask about accommodation. Everywhere was fully booked – hostels, campsites and all but the most expensive hotels – the reason being that the Dalai Lama was in town. There was no chance of me getting to see him, so I moved on.

It was a dull day from start to finish and the prospect of camping didn't appeal as I cycled in the direction of Martigny. The hillsides to my left were covered in acres of neat vineyards and I couldn't help wondering why I'd never seen Swiss wine in England. I assumed they drank it all themselves and later discovered I was right – Switzerland only exports 2% of its wine production. I wish I'd tried it now. I found a hotel just outside Vevey, and, even with a little haggling, paid more than I wanted to. Hopefully, living expenses would reduce once I left Western Europe.

I set out the next day in fabulous sunshine and air so clear, it almost hurt the eyes. The sky was deep blue and the mountains of the Alps were topped with fluffy white clouds. In Vevey, I stopped at a market beside Lake Geneva, to buy a large punnet of cherries and a bag of plums. At a jewellery stall, I bought a silver ring which would come in useful if for any reason I needed to say I was married. On the tidy car park, vendors tempted visitors with linen, carpets and furniture, and a flower display of sunflowers dazzled the eye. As I squeezed among the crowds, an English tourist stopped to admire my loaded bike. He dropped into the conversation that he'd ridden the length of Britain, from John o' Groats on the northern tip of Scotland to Land's End in southwest England. I couldn't help thinking how much more his story would have impressed me at one time. He didn't ask what my ultimate goal was, so I didn't tell him.

With the clean mountain air in my lungs, I followed signs for Montreux and found a convenient bench beside the lake where I could sit comfortably and raid my panniers. I couldn't have been happier: 'This is what it's all about,' I thought. 'Having lunch in the sunshine on the side of Lake Geneva with not a care in the world'. Living on the edge of the English Lake District as I do, the scenery was reminiscent of home. It was my first visit to Switzerland and I loved it.

On the road to Martigny, I almost took a wrong turn onto the motorway and received abuse from an impatient driver. "You should pay more attention!" he shouted. He disappeared up the road, and, while I was thinking of all the smart retorts I could have given, a lady motorist slowed down beside me, wagged her finger and pointed me in the right direction. Once on the correct road, cycling was easy and mainly on dedicated cycle lanes along the valley bottom. The summer was progressing and orchards heavy with apricots, pears and apples lay to my left and right. The apricots were ripe and could be bought very cheaply at the roadside.

Looking back on this part of the journey, I must have been subconsciously mis-reading the map in order to stay in the lovely Rhône Valley. In Martigny, I should have taken the road to the Grand St Bernard Pass which would have led me to Aosta in Italy, but, blinded by the beauty of the scenery and enjoying the ease of the cycling, I missed the turning. By the time I realised my mistake, I was content to continue on, even though I was heading towards the much steeper Simplon Pass.

When Sion came into view it took my breath away. To either side, the backdrop of the immense heights of the Bernese Alps created a scene straight from Mervyn Peake's Gormenghast trilogy. Its twin landmarks, the 12th century Basilique de Valère and the Château de Tourbillon, rise up each on its own rocky outcrop, created by the glaciers that carved the great Rhône Valley. I drank in the vista and then went to find a hostel.

It was mid-afternoon and the only person on duty was Marcel, a student volunteer. He was eager to help but couldn't book me in and offered to store my bike and bags until 5pm when the 'Chief' would be back. I took him up on his suggestion and walked into town to climb up the quiet Rue des Châteaux to the base of the two peaks. The Château claims to own the oldest playable organ in the world, dating from 1390. It is still in use and played every Saturday during July and August as part of the International Festival of Ancient Music. The charm of these ancient buildings lies mainly in their castellated exteriors. I wandered around the walls and then walked back down the hill to enjoy a relaxing coffee and a beer, before making my way back to the hostel. Bad news greeted me on my arrival. Marcel had been unaware that all the rooms were full. There was a large party of cyclists staying and not a bed to spare. 'Mon Dieu!' I thought, or something stronger in English. But all was not lost – when the 'Chief' heard what had happened, he offered me floor space in the staff accommodation in the loft. I had no desire to go hunting for a campsite by then and was glad to accept, although I was a bit miffed when he charged me the price of a dorm bed. Still, I was glad to be under cover, and settled myself in before walking back to the town centre, where I thought it was only fair to treat myself to a Thai red curry and a couple more beers.

Towards the end of the valley, I had my first experience of cycling through a tunnel. Staying on the road in a tunnel terrifies me and walking on the narrow sidewalks requires serious concentration because they are usually badly maintained. I walked deliberately and steadily along the slippery footpath, watching every step in the blackness. Halfway along, an echoing voice behind me made me jump and I turned to see another cyclist appearing out of the gloom, wanting to pass. He looked supremely confident, but I couldn't wait to reach the exit and as time went on, tunnels would be something I'd learn to dread.

At the foot of the Alps, I stayed in the lovely town of Brig, the central hub of a series of rail routes. I could have taken the train which takes you through the Simplon tunnel to Italy, but for me, this wasn't an option; I had to somehow get over the pass under my own steam.

Switzerland

Pushing over the Alps

Crossing the Simplon Pass was going to be my biggest challenge yet, and in the morning I stocked up with lots of fluids before setting off. The road started to climb and it wasn't long before I had to get off and push. Five miles on, the route was signed in green and I wasn't sure whether it was open to cyclists or not. There was no one to ask and I knew that if I returned to Brig to find out, I'd end up taking the easy option through the tunnel, because I wouldn't be able to face repeating the climb I'd just done. With fingers crossed, I got on to the Simplon road, and, hoping for the best, resolved to make out I didn't speak any French if stopped by the police (which was mostly true). No cars blared at me or shouted abuse, which was promising, but there was no hard shoulder and I was pushing all the time.

After a couple of hours in the sweltering heat, I climbed over a crash barrier and flopped onto a shady patch of grass. Ten minutes rest and I was cooled down and ready to continue. I'd also seen cyclists coming the other way, so I was feeling more reassured and carried on until the next picnic spot, where I stopped for lunch at a shady stone table.

The rest of the day was spent in a similar fashion, pushing and stopping at shorter and shorter intervals to catch my breath. As I climbed higher, glimpses of the ever-diminishing town of Brig below me came regularly into view. Halfway up the pass, the Ganter Bridge crossed the Ganter River and at almost 700 metres long, it gave me some respite from the incline of the mountainside road.

In spite of my slow progress, I was gaining height and it wasn't long before I was looking down on the 150 metre high concrete bridge. Through one tunnel after another – one of them two kilometres long – I pushed and pushed. Some of them weren't enclosed tunnels but vaulted galleries open on the precipitous outer side, while they hugged the rocks on my left. In one, the rock face disappeared into pitch blackness. I could hear the sound of rushing water and make out the shadows of a waterfall in the darkness. A fenced gap had been left between the rock face and the road to allow the water to take its natural course – it was quite beautiful as it sparkled in the thin light within the gloom. The day wore on and my right foot started to ache from the strain of constantly walking and pushing my heavy load at an angle. I tried swapping sides but that wasn't an option. I seem to be a 'right-handed pusher' and found it difficult to steer from the left.

Eight hours on and sixteen miles from the start, I reached the summit at 2005 metres. It was 6pm and I stopped to enjoy the magnificent panorama of the Bernese Alps. The view of the majestic snow-capped peaks was impressive, but one of the best sights for me was a road sign pointing to Italy and warning trucks to beware of their brakes overheating during the twenty-three kilometres of downhill! A sight to gladden the eyes – and the legs.

The steep descent proved to be more stressful than I'd expected. I was now riding on the road and competing with traffic – and the tunnels on the downhill side were terrifying at speed. I crossed the Italian border through the stunning Gondo Gorge, hemmed in by imposing granite walls, but I didn't have much chance to enjoy it at the speed I was going. As I flew down the mountain, it started to rain and I heard thunder in the distance. At the first opportunity, I stopped at a gas station to don waterproofs, look for maps and let my brakes cool down.

By now, the day had deteriorated and the light was fading. Domodossola, my original goal was too far away, so following a sign, I peeled off in the direction of a village to look for a bed. In Varso, I took a room in a hotel with a price that suited me; the furniture was shabby but the sheets were clean, and from the balcony I could watch the gathering storm roll down the Ossola Valley I'd just left.

Italy

Sweltering in the Heat

Italy immediately presented me with my first major language hurdle. I can struggle along in French, and have a few words of German and Russian, but Italian – nonno! I unpacked my panniers, had a shower and went to the restaurant across the road, where I was faced with a frosty waitress who had little patience with a non-lingo speaker. The pork pasta dish I thought I'd ordered turned out to be a large pork chop on a plate and nothing else. It was tasty enough, but not what I expected, and the waitress, who must have known, showed no sympathy. If I could have told her how far I'd travelled, would she have been more helpful? – who knows?

It was raining the next morning and the included breakfast was minimal – one croissant and a coffee – no joy there. I set off kitted out in waterproofs and a few miles along the road, bumped into three Canadian cyclists who invited me to join them cycling into Domodossola. They were much younger than me and I knew I'd never keep up, so we arranged to meet for coffee in town, where we enjoyed an hour talking about our trips. They left ahead of me and I followed at my slower pace.

How different Italy was from clean, crisp Switzerland. The roads deteriorated as soon as I crossed the border and the buildings were visibly in need of repair. Whether it was due to a change in culture, climate or economics was too soon to say, but I got the impression the locals would rather sit in the sun than mend the roof.

I had planned to camp in Verbania but no suitable campsite appeared near the town centre and instead I made an early crossing of Lake Maggiore. As I wheeled onto the ferry with a huge raspberry 'gelato' in my left hand, steering my bike with the right and my left elbow, who should turn up again but the Canadians.

We crossed to Laveno where we found accommodation and spent a convivial evening together, chatting about our backgrounds and the climb over the Simplon Pass. Carol-Anne and her brother had pedalled the whole sixteen miles and I was feeling embarrassingly feeble, until their companion said he'd taken the train through the tunnel.

After saying goodbye to my Canadian friends in the morning, I left Laveno and headed for Como – thirteen manageable miles, then another twelve or so of stiff uphills, with the rest pretty much downhill. It was now the middle of August, and the heat of the day had become almost unbearable. I sweated proverbial buckets on most days. The suntan cream on my forehead ran into my eyes and smarted, and as fast as I mopped my skin, the more it continued to stream. My shirt clung to me, like – well, like clingfilm.

I'd promised myself another gelato as soon as the shops opened in the afternoon and when I screeched to a halt outside an ice-cream shop in Como, the proprietor's smiling face was a picture – as I'm sure was mine. In spite of my lack of Italian, I knew exactly what he was saying to his wife - "Just come and look at this..." – me that is, red in the face, melting with the heat and on a bicycle carrying a load that looks like madness to many. I took it all in good humour, as I propped up my bike and stepped into the chill of their air-conditioned ice-cream palace – bliss!

In the height of summer, Lake Como is full of tourists and hotel prices are sky high, but on enquiring at the tourist information I was told there was a youth hostel in the town with beds available. The dorm was very pleasant – spacious with a view across the lake, but the included breakfast was one of the poorest I'd had – white bread and jam, and warm coffee served with a ladle. I ate what I could, and left crowded Como for Bergamo which looked far more interesting – another old town sitting high on a rocky outcrop.

That evening I wrote in my diary:-

> *"The days seem to belong to a different time zone. It's hard to believe that such a lot happens in one day. This morning I was in Como – tonight in Bergamo. Different to driving. Such a lot happens in between. You feel like it takes days – not hours. So many experiences."*

From the beautiful streets and churches of Bergamo, I continued on to Verona. As time went on, I realised I was getting better at handling very busy traffic. Instead of pedalling like billy-o to get out of the mayhem, repeating to myself, 'they're not allowed to kill me', – which is true, but not really the best premise to work on, I had started slowing down, giving myself lots of time to pull over and make decisions. In spite of this, the stress of highways and city traffic was taking its toll on my nerves, and eventually I veered off the direct route to take a quieter road. This wasn't a total success either. I was taken through unattractive industrial areas and flat, monotonous cornfields where there was no shade for most of the day, resulting in a seriously sunburned face. At one point, I pulled into a filling station with sweat pouring off me and badly in need of a cold drink. All I could do was mime drinking to the attendant and say the word "freddo?" (cold). The answer was "no", but I was so steamed up, that she gave me cup, after cup of water from her own fridge.

Verona is famous for being the setting of Shakespeare's 'Romeo and Juliet.' The balcony, which hangs from a 14th-century house and purports to be 'Juliet's balcony', is fictional in every sense. Shakespeare never visited the city but instead took his story from a local legend. It doesn't deter tourists from wanting to see it, and be photographed caressing the bronze statue of Juliet suggestively (her left breast is rubbed shiny.)

The city is also famous for its Roman amphitheatre. Completed around 30 AD, it is the third-largest in Italy and could seat some 25,000 spectators in its forty-four tiers of marble seats. It was once the scene of gladiator games, but only a fragment of the original outer perimeter wall, in beautiful white and rose limestone from Valpolicella, remains. I believe the interior is very impressive and is virtually intact. It was hosting the annual opera festival while I was there, and I wasn't able to see it without a ticket.

I enjoyed Verona, but for me the jewel in Italy lay further east, in a more modest and less famous town. South of the cities of Venezia and Padua, the scenery was again less than inspiring, but when I reached my next destination, the dreary miles were forgotten. Montagnana dates back to Roman times and is encircled by perfectly-preserved medieval city walls. The Gothic fortress of a cathedral in the town square is decorated inside with beautiful frescoes, paintings and polished stonework. The town is so unspoiled it was hard to understand why it wasn't thronging with visitors. I needed at least a day to explore this fine town and booked in for two nights at the hostel.

The streets were packed that evening with people of all ages, youngsters, grandparents and families with children, for a festival culminating in, of all things, bingo at midnight! In the square, a stage had been erected and strains of Eric Clapton filled the air. I stayed long enough to see a live band perform, but by 10pm, the prospect of bingo wasn't enough to keep me awake and I retired to my room. The next day was spent walking the city walls, exploring the alleyways and old buildings, and sampling the local speciality dish, Montagnana ham.

That night I was kept awake by a loud funfair and in an attempt to block out the noise, I found my earplugs and ducked under the covers. The commotion stopped around midnight but

I was still awake and took out the earplugs. Calamity! The left one broke apart and a piece of silicon was stuck fast in my ear canal. Any attempts I made to extract it, only made things worse and I knew I would need medical attention.

In the morning I went to the nearby local hospital, where a doctor examined my ear. The silicon was so firmly lodged that he told me I would need to go to the next town, Este, to see a specialist. He was in the process of advising me on transport, when I explained that I would be cycling there because it was on my route. The doctor looked at me as if I was quite mad. "You cannot cycle" he said, "it's twenty kilometres to Este". As the story of my travels unfolded, every answer I gave prompted amused disbelief and then comments of admiration.

"You have cycled from England?"

"Yes, (well, Calais)."

"How many miles?"

"Over a thousand."

"Are you alone?"

"Yes."

"Are you going back to England?"

"No – Slovenia."

"Are you going to write a book?"

"Possibly…"

He finally understood that cycling was by far my best option and as we shook hands, he said, "Be careful of the trucks". I was grateful for his concern, but secretly wondered how I'd managed to get as far as this with so many similar warnings.

Este was sixteen miles away and the hospital was easy to find. The Montagnana doctor had rung ahead and it didn't take long to be seen. An ear specialist syringed my ear and flushed out a plug of silicon as big as a pea. It had felt like a golf ball to me. I showed my European Health Insurance Card but there was no charge. I assumed it wasn't worth the paperwork.

In two days, I would reach Venice and I planned to take some time off and make a short holiday of it. I was ready for a break. The weather had been in the high thirties for a few days and was forecast to hit forty degrees. I stopped under the shade of a tree on the way to Chioggia, again sweating faster than I could mop. An elderly man appeared just as I approached my next shady stop under a tree and we exchanged our "Buonjournos". I could see he lived in the nearby house and as I was muttering under my breath that he might have offered me a cold drink, he came back – and offered me a cold drink. Neither of us spoke the other's language, but when he said "aqua?"(water) and I said "freddo?" (cold), we had it cracked. I followed him down the track to his house and he brought a container of water out of his fridge and filled up my bottle again and again as I drained it. His wife appeared and chattered in Italian about how "caldo" (hot) it was, while I sweated and nodded. As I left, he handed me peaches from one of his trees and would have loaded my panniers up with more if I hadn't made 'too heavy' gestures. Yet another lesson in the kindness of human nature.

Chioggia is a charming town at the southern end of the Venetian lagoon, and when I arrived, the only hostel was full. It was now the height of the season and at the tourist information office I was directed to a campsite on Sottomarina, an adjacent island linked by a system of bridges. It remains memorable to me for its absence of any charm whatsoever. It was heaving with tourists, and along the length of the seafront, campsites, water parks and seaside vendors proliferated – the sort of place of my worst nightmare. On a site in an enclosure beside the road, I was shown to a pitch, bare of grass and separated from the traffic by nothing more than a woven plastic fence. Not surprisingly, I declined. Leaving Sottomarina as swiftly as possible, I cycled back to Chioggia and found a hotel.

Two island strips border the east side of the Venetian Lagoon. The first, Pellestrina, is eleven kilometres long and only half a kilometre wide in places. I caught the ferry to Pellestrina and had a pleasant ride to its northern tip, before taking another ferry to the second of the bordering islands, Lido de Venezia. I had planned to stay in a hostel in Venice but one thing that had escaped me was that cycles are not allowed on its islands. On realising this, I was left with no option but to stay in Lido and see Venice city by waterbus.

As I pushed my bike along the main street of upmarket Lido, I must have presented a strange sight to the rest of the tourists in their shorts and sundresses. I approached a number of two-star hotels and was turned away with an unconvincing "sorry – full". Should I have a wash, change my clothes and try to look like some of the fashionistas strolling around town? That was never going to happen. Looking further, I found an information point where I was given a list of hotels to ring and there was no problem finding a room over the phone. Hotel La Meridiana may have been less than pleased when the dusty, sweaty cyclist arrived with her bike and cargo, but I was booked in and they didn't turn me away.

Venice in the middle of July is anything but relaxing, and one day visiting the main sights among the crowds was enough for me. I made a short trip the next morning to the north of the islands to investigate the quieter parts. The city is undoubtedly beautiful, but in the end, I found the beach on Lido much more restful. Perhaps a return visit out of season is in order.

I wouldn't like anyone to think that I am seeing the world through rose-tinted spectacles, so here I'd like to redress the balance of my reports of meeting many helpful, interesting and kind people. I also met a lot of rude ones, and some places have a lot to learn in the customer service area. On one of the boat trips I took around Venice, I decided to buy a bite to eat from the bar. What I thought looked like a nice soft roll turned out to be a lot less than soft when I picked it up, having paid my 3.50 euros. As is my wont in these circumstances, I told the barman that the roll was not good, it was dry and stale. The response I got was "It is good – maybe for you it's not good – for me it's good." When I pointed out that I was the customer, he took the roll and slapped it under a panini iron and gave it back to me. Unbelievable – or am I just one of those awkward foreigners?

Another incident happened in Lido when I picked up a punnet of peaches on a fruit stall. The owner spoke to me very rudely and told me that there were other customers in front of me and I should take a numbered ticket. He knew I was English because he had served me the day before without a problem when custom was slow and I hadn't realised there was a ticketing system.

I was prodded rudely on the shoulder when I was queuing for a boat ticket because I hadn't put my bike in the holding area, and I was regularly spoken to with obvious impatience because I don't speak the language. It was my first visit to Italy and I came across many, many nice people. It's just a shame that the impolite ones give such a bad impression.

Anyway, I'll get off my soapbox and climb back on the saddle…

Well-rested after three days, I left the Hotel Meridiana and headed for the ferry to Punta Sabbioni. I was sorry to miss saying goodbye to my young friend Jack, who had kept me company in the hotel lounge as we were using the internet. Our conversations on computing and Italy and my trip, (which he was extremely interested in, even though he thought I was "mental") had entertained me for many an hour.

From the ferry, I cycled off in the direction of Slovenia, with that now familiar feeling that I was saying goodbye to a country and it was time to concentrate on the next.

Jesolo on the mainland was much less frantic. Shops lined the main highway, but there were fewer visitors and following the cycle lanes was easy – until I reached the tail-end of a traffic jam. The hold-up turned out to be five miles long and for the next hour I was able to skirt along the inside of the cars, to the obvious displeasure of some of the drivers, who were mostly at a standstill. I cleared the queue of traffic and continued on my now peaceful ride.

When I reached Latisana, I felt I could probably make it to the next hostel at Aquileia, so I rang up and booked myself in. It was a further twenty-five miles and turned out to be not the best decision. After fifteen miles, I'd had enough and the last ten were a struggle, mainly caused by 'rear-ache'.

Since Verona, my Brooks saddle had been causing me trouble. I now had 1500 miles on the clock and the leather was still as rock-hard as new, in spite of being oiled conscientiously, as per the supplier's instructions. Some of the online cycle forums recommended giving it a good thrashing with a blunt instrument, whereas other cyclists thought that would be a travesty. I was beginning to think it might be a good idea.

By the time I arrived in Aquileia at around 6.45pm, I was exhausted and couldn't wait to get off the bike. I checked into the hostel, was in bed by 8pm and slept soundly until 7am.

Slovenia

Imaginary Wolves

What two words spring to mind when describing Slovenia? For me, they are 'verdant' and 'friendly'. After the flat plains of northern Italy, it was a pleasure to find myself among the green hills, pastures and meadows of my fourth country, and among the welcoming Slovenian people. In the supermarkets, they were happy to cut off a chunk of bread from a large loaf. This was customer service at its best.

As usual, I'd worked out my route through Eastern Europe using the truly scientific, lengthy, research method I'd been employing all along – i.e. – draw a straight line between A and B and see how close I could get to it on the map. So, I had Goriza on the Italian border at the A end, and Sofia in Bulgaria at the B end, (highly technical this, hope you're keeping up), with lots of Balkan countries in between.

In spite of my love of the more rugged terrain, after three days I'd cursed a thousand times the many hills I pushed up. The road to Cerknica took me through a lonely, gloomy wood, and try as I might, I couldn't help thinking about Dervla Murphy's encounter with wolves, when she cycled from Dunkirk to Delhi in 1963, and used her revolver for the first time in the Balkans. My nerves had been primed earlier, when I passed through a village called Volce Draga and was informed by a local that it translated to "Wolf Valley". I struggled uphill, becoming more and more spooked by the silence and worked out my strategy in case a wolf leapt out of the undergrowth. I would immediately turn and fly back downhill. All complete nonsense of course, but it's funny how the mind plays tricks in such situations.

Clearing the wood and surviving the imaginary wolves, I reached a T-junction and could see that to my left was a very steep incline uphill, and to the right, an impressive downhill. It was time to stop in a nearby bar and have a rest. I sipped my coffee slowly, studied my map and ventured out to reassess. No excuses – it had to be left and uphill. After two exhausting miles, the crest of the last hill was gained and I climbed back on the saddle. When the scenery opened up, I knew that slogging up those hills had been worth every drop of sweat. Nova Vas – a town so lovely in its isolation; a small farming enclave nestling in a glorious setting; a magical place situated on a plateau at the top of a mountain range, with a population of under three hundred people. Fields radiated from the edges of the settlement to the encircling foothills – another unspoiled gem to add to my collection.

At Bloke Ranch farm, I saw the word for rooms 'soba' and stopped to find the proprietor. An elderly woman appeared who spoke no English. "Un momento" she said, and rang her granddaughter on a mobile phone. A room was arranged and, after settling in, I walked to the village shop to find supper. I bought bread, meat paste, a slice of watermelon and a bottle of Slovenian wine, all the ingredients for a very pleasant evening writing my diary.

Next morning, the air was crisp and clear when I surveyed the glorious vista in its morning dress and I was reluctant to leave my idyllic haven. Grandfather, who was German, greeted me and we managed a few pleasantries over tea and biscuits, while Grandma and I shared photos of our children. The conversation soon flagged and my cycling trip was broached. "Macedonia?" Grandma enquired. I brought out my map to show her where I was going, at which she gasped and muttered something I didn't understand. I suspected she thought me quite mad. As I was leaving, another granddaughter, who spoke good English, arrived with her husband. "Are you alone?" they asked. My answer was relayed to the grandparents, giving rise to more gasps of amazement. I asked if Grandma thought I was mad. "Yes," said the granddaughter, "but she thinks that about a lot of things". "Take care" said Grandma as I pedalled off – one of the few phrases I remembered reading in my mostly-useless phrasebook.

It was a good road out of Nova Vas and the Slovenians are considerate drivers when it comes to giving cyclists plenty of room, especially the truck drivers. The road surface continued to be even, until I made the mistake of taking a short cut. Ten miles later, a sign appeared saying, 'No asphalt', and for a further three miles, I bumped along the gravel in the middle of a forest, once again watching out for wolves. Naïvely, I expected to reach road works at some point, but there were none, the sign was just a warning. The other disadvantage of taking the shorter route, was that it took me through small hamlets with no accommodation, and I was fast becoming anxious about where I would be spending the night.

At the small border town Vinica, I asked around for anyone with rooms, or even the remote possibility of a hotel, but there was nothing. I was feeling tired and despondent when I went into the village shop to buy a drink, and without much hope, asked again. Good news – there was a nearby campground, and within half an hour, I was pitched and making tea. It was to be my last night in a tent for many months to come.

Croatia

Missing my Greens

Croatia wasn't yet a member of the EU, so the first thing I needed was currency. I made for the nearest large town Karlovac to find a bank and collect my kunas.

I'm sure many parts of the country are very beautiful, especially along the Adriatic Coast, but the north had had little money invested since the war. A hotel I passed was nothing but a shell, presumably a casualty of the Croatian War of Independence. Houses were peppered with bullet holes, some of them patched with cement, but many untouched. New dwellings on the outskirts of towns were unfinished, but obviously occupied. I stopped at a café hoping to find something to eat, but despite the fact that it could have seated over a hundred customers, there was only one other and I could only buy coffee. I wondered how it managed to stay open.

On the way out of Karlovac, I found a room in a private house and the next day left for Glina. As I was leaving, the landlady asked why I was going there, "is it for something interesting?" When I asked what was wrong with it, she shrugged and said, "Well, it is in a national park", as if it had little else to offer.

I could understand the landlady's question when I reached Glina. It was not a pretty town. Houses with collapsed roofs and smashed windows were constant reminders of the war. Men sat outside cafés and eyed me suspiciously as I walked along the streets. The Hotel Cassina was clean and tidy but the food was basic. I ordered vegetable soup from the menu and was served a clear broth with noodles in it; not many vitamins there. The main course was a badly cooked trout which had obviously lain in a freezer for months, and a few chips. I didn't finish either course. An internet café in the town made up for the lack of wifi in the hotel, but it was a dilapidated place, with shabby furniture and a patched, pitted floor. Old bits of worn carpet were used to little effect and the paintwork was bright but dirty.

That evening, a cavalcade of cars drove down the main street outside my window, with flags and ribbons waving and horns honking. I wondered if it was a political demonstration, but it turned out to be simply a wedding party.

In spite of my less than cheerful surroundings, I was ready for a rest and stayed two nights, giving me time to study my map and plan the next part of the route. I had planned to travel east to Serbia, but there didn't seem to be a way round the main A3 highway north of the border. If instead, I entered Bosnia at Dubica, I could cross to Serbia at Zvornic, from where a diagonal route would take me to Sofia. It seemed like a better plan.

Bosnia

A Tussle in Tuzla

The River Sava flows through Slovenia and Croatia, along the northern border of Bosnia and Herzegovina and through Serbia's capital Belgrade, where it discharges into the Danube. I reached the border around midday and had lunch on the banks of the river, before crossing the bridge linking the two countries. The Bosnian guard waved me through with a smile.

There was a noticeable difference in the air on the Bosnian side, with signs of prosperity in stark evidence. Elaborate houses dotted the countryside and even the more modest dwellings were surrounded with high-quality stainless steel railings. Colourful rugs hung from balconies and music played. New builds under construction and modern factories and farming equipment were signs of a thriving economy. People were friendly and helpful despite the language barrier and most took my presence as unremarkable.

Cycling along the river plain, I reached Dubica by late afternoon and was surprised to find there was no hotel in this sizeable town. One woman tried to help but spoke no English, so we both gave up. I wandered on through the main street and stopped at a bar. The barmaid also spoke no English but referred me to a customer who did. Unfortunately, as he talked, I was unable to look him in the face – a face full of rotten teeth and nasal debris. He told me of a motel on the outskirts of town and then went on to offer me his spare room for twenty-five marks. I found it very easy to decline his offer politely and headed for the motel.

I left the next day in good spirits and thought of England as I rode past neat irregular-shaped pastures stretching off to the horizon, where Friesian cows grazed and wildflowers grew. Fields of ripened corn stood ready for harvesting. Old-style hayricks standing in the meadows and Orthodox churches with ornate cupolas reminded me that no, I was not at home.

The main road south to Banja Luka was very busy, with little more than a sheep track for a cycle path beside the road for a number of miles. The truck drivers beeped at me if I didn't use it, so I was pleased when I reached a newly-paved section with wheel ramps at the kerbs. A mile later the new path finished, when the road workers who were laying it appeared, and I was back on the main road. Traffic management was non-existent: no cones, no barriers, no traffic lights; vehicles simply worked their way around the workmen and heavy plant. If there was a digger in the middle of the carriageway, the drivers managed themselves.

In a bookshop in Duboj, I bought a 'Serbian for Foreigners' phrasebook and pushed my bike through the streets looking for the only hotel in town. On the way, I met a family of three with a story which is all too common in this part of the world. The brother and sister were Bosnian and had just been reunited for the first time in seventeen years. Their family was torn apart during the Yugoslav war and the sister had escaped to Germany, losing all contact with her relatives. She had married a German and he was there with her. I would have like to hear the whole story but even though they were also staying at the same hotel as me, I sadly didn't see them again

Duboj is a large bustling town with wide roads and a central park lined with trees. Its appearance is marred by the buildings which are post-Communist in style and box-like. Some of them still carry the marks of war damage but there is little on the faces of the inhabitants to remind you. Walking out before dinner, I strolled among families enjoying the public spaces, boys playing football, others rollerblading around the park paths, young parents with babies in prams, and cooing grannies. It was a wonderful atmosphere in the evening light.

The hotel was fairly luxurious and at breakfast I thought I'd died and gone to heaven. I'd ordered bacon and eggs and got a fair approximation of English bacon, and two beautifully fried eggs with fluffy whites and runny yolks. It had been a while.

Leaving Doboj in the direction of Tuzla, I came upon a clearing at the side of the road which was covered in smooth rocks of varying sizes. The time had come to tackle the posterior problem. I was getting to the point where thirty miles was about as much as I could do in a day because the saddle was so uncomfortable, so I picked up a large rock, and gave the seat a hammering, making sure I had treated all areas evenly. It left a few scuff marks, but after another oiling, it looked no worse than the more expensive 'antique' leather model. I climbed aboard and immediately felt a difference. The leather was now giving under my sit-bones and my weight was being distributed evenly. It was a vast improvement and I was glad I hadn't left the assault any longer.

Later in the day, I was flagged down by two French cyclists going the opposite way and we stood chatting, exchanging information. When we parted, I was feeling mentally refreshed from my roadside encounter and carried on in a bright mood to Tuzla, where the day was about to take a downturn.

The land around Tuzla could in no way be described as attractive. The activities of the mining industry have ravaged the area and left it with severe subsidence problems. Extractions of the city's salt deposits have caused sections of the centre to sink and structures in the sinking area have either collapsed or been demolished. There are few left that predate the 20th century. The only place I saw advertising rooms was a down-at-heel establishment, and I turned it down to look elsewhere. As I cycled through the city centre, I was jeered at from a distance by a youth in a café. He seemed to find a cyclist riding a fully-loaded bike an object of derision and I rode on feeling decidedly annoyed. Fifteen minutes later, I pushed my bike up a steep hill on the way out of town and passed a group of children no more than ten years of age. The ringleader ('probably the child of the half-wit in town', I thought) started showing off to her friends by pointing and laughing loudly at me as I sweated up the hill. The day was not going well and continued on its downward slide as I passed villages where school buses were unloading and more children started cat-calling me. Young men driving dilapidated cars blared their horns at me in derision. There was no mistaking the contempt. What was happening? I was now vexed and decided to make an early run for the Serbian border, keeping an eye out for somewhere to stay. It was 6pm and daylight was fading when I checked in at the first hotel, glad to get off the road and away from the hostility I'd been experiencing.

The hotel was shabby and I was the only guest, but I had a first-rate meal in the restaurant and the staff were friendly. The next morning, as I checked out, the manager appeared and couldn't do enough to help me load my bike, mainly getting in the way, but all well-intended. I didn't want to let my experience in Tuzla colour my view of a country in which I'd generally had a very happy time, so I decided to put yesterday's unpleasantness aside.

With my spirits improving and back on track, I set off for the Serbian border.

Serbia

Staying in Room 101

It was a shock to cross into Serbia and hit a badly-patched, cobbled road leading to the border town of Loznica. Things didn't get much better in the town itself, with broken pavements, buildings in disrepair and pollution hanging in the air. There was only one place to stay, and it was a swish, western-style hotel, sitting incongruously in the centre of town. Rooms were expensive and the receptionist flatly refused to find a safe place for my bike. "You must leave your bicycle in the car park", she said. I thought about demanding to see the manager, but wasn't too sure I wanted to pay their price anyway. Instead, I asked if there was any other accommodation in town or on the Valjevo road and was told I would find someone with rooms at Zavlaka, thirteen kilometres away.

Disappointment awaited in Zavlaka when my request for "Hotel?" brought forth blank looks. The locals could only suggest I carry on to Osečina, the next town a further fifteen kilometres on.

Halfway to Osečina, I cycled past a parked truck and noticed the driver stood behind, taking a pee. I rode on thinking no more of it until he overtook me and pulled up a few yards ahead. This seemed a little odd and when he called to me from the cab, my instincts told me he was up to no good. I ignored him and pedalled on and it wasn't long before he set off and drove past me again. His behaviour was beginning to concern me now, so I stopped at the gate of a house where a family sat outside. The mother came over to see if I needed help but she spoke no

English and as the truck disappeared round a bend in the road, I tried to explain with gestures that that the driver was harassing me. Unsurprisingly, she didn't understand so I changed the subject and asked about rooms (sobe) in Osečina. This brought forth a positive response as if there was somewhere to stay.

We carried on conversing for a further few minutes, with me pointing at the sun and smiling and the woman pointing at my bike with admiration, then I set off. As I turned the bend, there was the truck parked up. I was now convinced the driver was a threat, but there was enough traffic and habitation along the route to reassure me that I wasn't in too much danger. With some trepidation, I cycled towards the vehicle, expecting the driver to talk to me again, but as I approached, he walked out of the trees on my right and said something again in Serbian. Now I was alarmed and pedalled as fast as I could, praying I wouldn't have to get off for any hills. A minute later he appeared behind me again and stayed there, crawling at my speed of twelve miles an hour. This went on for a couple of minutes and I decided it was time to take action. I waited for some cars to come the other way and crossing in front of the truck, stopped in the middle of the road to wave them down. The cars slowed down and the truck driver shot past on my right, disappearing into the distance ahead. The oncoming vehicles didn't actually stop, but the truck driver had gone for good.

Osečina was characteristic of most of the towns I saw in Serbia. In the streets, men of all ages sat outside café-bars drinking beer, with seemingly little else to do. Buildings and roads were badly in need of repair, but the economy obviously didn't allow for improvements. Outside most commercial establishments, stood transparent-fronted fridges stocked with beer. In some ways, it was a depressing impression, but in the same breath it was refreshing to see the absence of Western excesses. Eastern Europeans are very friendly and helpful and this part of the world remains one of my favourite destinations.

Again, I was met everywhere with blank looks at the word "Hotel?" and found very little English spoken until a girl in a bar informed me, "There is a wo-man" (I remember she pronounced the 'o' as in no). She made a phone call and directed me to a house where Ivana, an elderly lady, greeted me warmly. She had been recently widowed and was obviously eager for company. Her sprawling property had been extended to incorporate three flats which she rented out. She showed me into one of them but it was crammed full of sofas and there was no sign of a bed. Seeing my hesitation, she next offered me her spare room in the main house. I wasn't too sure about this, because each time I asked, "How much?" she avoided the question. In the end, I pushed her for an answer. "Nothing dolling" she said, "I don't want paying".

I stayed with Ivana for three nights and spent many hours listening to her fascinating life story. Some of it was spent with her children in Austria and Australia, so she had learned to speak German and English, although much had been forgotten over the years. Our conversations were a jumble of English, German and Serbian, and with my few words of German and Russian, we were able to communicate quite well.

The evenings were spent in her cosy sitting room, hulling hazelnuts as she told me about her youth. Born in Montenegro in 1930 during WWII, she hid in a tree at the age of eleven and watched while most of her family perished in their burning house. She was taken by the military to an orphanage and was later shot during the conflict, sustaining wounds which left three pieces of shrapnel in her back. Her older brother and sister had escaped the fire but died later in the military. In later life, she'd had two heart operations and a hip replacement. She told me that during the Yugoslav wars, Osečina had got off lightly because of its remoteness, although she knew many people elsewhere who had died. In spite of the hardship she had suffered throughout her life, she never stopped smiling.

The house was bulging with bedding, towels, knick-knacks and clothes, much of it belonging to her late husband. Every surface was piled with mountains of linen. An extensive orchard lay at the back of the house stocked with fruit-laden trees. Inside the house, boxes of apples, pears and plums covered the floors, slowly decomposing and covered in fruit flies. The bread in the kitchen cupboards was also alive with tiny flies, but Ivana's failing eyesight wasn't good enough to see them. She could see house flies however, and as she cooked us a tasty Serbian stew, she sang and wielded a fly swat to good effect.

On my last day it was clear she would have liked me to stay longer, but knowing I'd never get away without making a firm stand, I thought it best to make my apologies and leave.

On the Sunday I took off in the direction of Arandjelovac, some sixty miles on, and again there was no sign of accommodation until I reached the town and saw arrowed signs pointing to 'Hotels' (note, in the plural). My hopes were rising, but soon to be dashed. The signs were old and there was only one hotel in town, the 'Sumadja', a sizeable rectangular building with echoes of George Orwell's '1984' inside and out. The interior looked as if it hadn't been redecorated for over fifty years. Giant iron radiators clung to the walls and everything up to waist height was covered in shiny dark brown paint with a dirty cream above. In the centre of the stairwell was an ancient cast iron lift, all of it painted shiny brown, and of course, out of order. I wasn't surprised to find that the room I'd been given was, indeed, Room 101.

At least I had a bed for the night, even if it wasn't the most luxurious, but there were more concerns to come. The manager asked me for a registration card, something I'd been given in the last hotel in Bosnia and was using as a bookmark in my phrasebook. The card presented a problem because I'd arrived in Serbia three days ago and didn't have anything to prove where I'd been for the previous two nights. I explained I'd been staying with Ivana and had her address and phone number with me. The manager was agitated by this and told me that in Serbia, you must stay at a hotel and receive a card each time, to show a record of your movements within the country. He then made a phone call to the police explaining the situation. I don't know if he rang Ivana, but thankfully there were no repercussions. The next morning, I was served a tasteless breakfast of bread and butter with jam, pink sausage paste, and warm tea. Before I left, the manager insisted on checking my onward route for hotels and instructing me to make sure I collected registration cards.

As is the luck of the independent cycling tourist, Ćuprija, my next stay, was a depressing town, with litter and dirt and weeds everywhere, and the next day, after only five miles, I passed through Paraćin with its spotlessly clean streets and a colourful street market. What a pity I hadn't pushed on a bit further.

Countryside roads in general were edged with litter and it was difficult finding somewhere to stop for a break. Dogs guarding properties barked at me as I rode past and strays were common.

I was chased by them more than once and saw a number of dead dogs on the road.

I hadn't been able to find a large scale map of Serbia and was using one of the Balkans, which wasn't that helpful. Leaving the town of Tešić, I realised after a few miles that I had taken a wrong turn. If I'd only listened to the woman who shouted to me at the top of her voice that I was going the wrong way and should go back and take the motorway, it might not have happened. She didn't appear to be the most reliable source of information, so I'd ignored her.

The road petered out at the head of a valley and I stopped at a farm to ask a group of men if this was the road to Niš (pronounced Nish). One of the men spoke good English and proceeded to draw me the most incomprehensible diagram with far too much detail. After some argument, his father intervened and drew three lines on the diagram, indicating I should go back to Tešić and turn right – which is what I did. Seventy-five arduous miles later I arrived in Niš and found my way to the Ambasador (sic) Hotel, where I booked in for three nights to rest my legs.

The first day was spent doing very little apart from relaxing and exploring the immediate vicinity. I'd made a decision before I left home to not bring any books with me. At the time, eBook readers were in their infancy and hard copies were the only real option. I had reasoned that at the start I would be too exhausted in the evenings to read, and in any case, weight restrictions meant I would only be able to take a couple, which wouldn't last long. I'd now spent two months in foreign-language countries and found myself hungry for reading material in English. As luck would have it, there was a bookshop beside my hotel that sold English novels. What a find.

The next day, I visited Skull Tower, a relic of the 1909 Serbian Uprising battle, after which the Turkish victor Vizier Hurshid Pasha built a tower and embedded the heads of 952 vanquished

Serbian soldiers into the mortar, as a warning to any potential adversaries. The tower, fifteen feet square and ten feet high, is now housed in a chapel just a little bigger than the tower itself. The skulls, many with cracks and holes in them, are a gruesome sight but I hate to think what the wall looked like when the heads were freshly positioned.

I returned to my hotel via the unlovely Church of the Emperor Constantine and Empress Helena, passing a lively street market where I bought a bag of plums and tried to offer the woman ten times what she was asking. £1.50 that is, instead of 15p – very embarrassing.

During the German occupation in World War II, the first Nazi concentration camp in Yugoslavia was located in Niš. A trip to the remains of the camp the next day proved to be a waste of time as there was nothing for the visitor to see. The perimeter fence was down in places and it looked as if the buildings inside were being used by businesses. I gave up and walked back to the hotel to plan my next move.

Online social networking sites were just becoming popular in 2009. One such site is Couchsurfing, which provides a contact hub for free homestays for its members. You can be a guest or a host without any money changing hands and the security is based on a reference system. This was a new experience for me and I tentatively registered with the website, to see if anyone in Sofia would be willing to put me up. Staying with a local person who could advise me about Sofia and Bulgaria itself was bound to be very useful. Within twenty-four hours, Petya and Ivo offered me a room in their attic for two nights. I was a little apprehensive, but it was a relief to know where I would be sleeping in my first capital city.

On the road out of Serbia, I passed a restaurant with a crowd of tourists milling round and stopped to spend my last dinars on a coffee. As I pulled in, a big bear of a man approached me with a look of wonder on his face. “Excuse me”, he said. “Can I ask you how old you are?" "I beg your pardon!" I answered, quite taken aback. "That's not a very gentlemanly question!" "But I'm just interested," he said, "because we don't see many ladies of your age riding bicycles". It was impossible to take umbrage with this friendly man, who was in no way trying to offend. I told him my age and we talked about the difference in western and eastern European customs. I would be asked the same question countless times in the following months.

And after all the fuss in the Sumadja hotel in Arandjelovac, the border crossing was without event, and no one wanted to see the precious movement cards I'd been religiously collecting.

Bulgaria

Disaster Strikes

The E80 highway runs from Niš to Sofia and I left Serbia, skirting the town of Dimitrovgrad and entering Bulgaria through narrow valleys flanked by tree-covered hills. On I cycled, until the hillsides opened up to the wide valley floor at the foot of Mount Vitosha, the scenic backdrop to the capital, Sofia. By late afternoon, I'd reached the outskirts of the capital where Romany encampments spread out to my right and horse-driven carts competed with the traffic. Further into the city, behind the shops, banks and hotels, rows of poorly maintained post-Communist apartment blocks appeared, and shiny, colourful gas stations rubbed shoulders with traditional cafés, some of them little more than shacks. As I rode, I looked out for the McDonald's restaurant where I'd arranged to meet my hosts.

Finding this symbol of western culture alive and well seemed strangely at odds with my earlier impressions of Eastern Europe. Inside, the fixtures and fittings were standard 'MacDee' and everything about the clientele was surprisingly familiar. Families wore western-style clothes and babies sat in western-style prams holding western-style toys. The relaxed atmosphere signified the kind of consumerism I hadn't seen since Italy. But whilst one section of society was relatively wealthy, it was evident from the earlier encampments, that there was another that had little. Bulgaria was proving to be a country of contradictions.

I crossed the road at the appointed time and saw a handsome young couple coming to greet me with broad smiles on their faces. In true gentlemanly manner, Ivo took the bike from me, while Petya, so pretty in her pigtails, chatted as we walked.

We made our way to a district of apartment blocks, like those that I'd seen earlier. This type of development was widely employed in communist Bulgaria between the 1950s and the 1980s. Constructed of large, prefabricated concrete slabs, many are now in bad repair, with peeling paint and cracked walls. Open areas in between, with their overgrown weeds and street dogs roaming loose, added to the general atmosphere of neglect. In contrast, a few of the blocks had been renovated externally, and I was pleased when we headed to one of these.

Through the entrance, concrete steps led up an echoing stairwell and once inside, Ivo opened a padlocked iron door to the basement where I could store my bike. We climbed the stairs to the top floor, passing apartments with similar iron doors giving nothing away as to what was behind. When Petya opened the outer security door on theirs, it was like stepping into another world. Behind a second wooden front door, a modern well-appointed residence was revealed and I was welcomed into a cosy, comfortable home.

My room in the attic above was a part of the property which Ivo had converted into a bedsit. Access was again through an iron door, but this one opened into the middle of a long dark passage, which initially was not so welcoming. At one end, a naked bulb shed a dim light on a second door, leading to my accommodation. At the opposite end, dusty rafters hung in heavy shadows. Thankfully, despite its bleak entrance, the living space inside the conversion was bright, comfortable and cheery and the décor had Petya's artistic touch stamped all over it.

That evening, I was treated to a traditional Bulgarian meal, a sign of the couple's generous hospitality. They both spoke good English and we talked until nine, when I made my excuses and retired to my bed. Leaving the comfort of their living room, I couldn't help but feel a certain amount of trepidation as I climbed the cold stairway alone and opened the heavy iron door.

The inner door had a key but the outer one wasn't locked and it resounded with a clang as it closed, adding to my unease. I shuddered and told myself not to be so silly but the dimly illuminated corridor still had me hoping an assailant wasn't hiding in the shadows behind me.

The following morning, I took a bus into the city centre to pick up a parcel from the Post Office and do some sightseeing.

I must have stood in every queue in the Post Office (and there were a few). The assistant behind the grille at the first counter directed me to another queue, where I was given a slip of paper and pointed to a third queue to get it stamped. Fifteen minutes passed before I reached that counter, where the assistant stamped the form and sent me back to the previous queue, to stand at the back of the line again. I presented the stamped paper to another assistant and after much discussion with her colleagues, my parcel was finally located. I later asked Ivo why the same person who issued the form couldn't have stamped it. "But the lady who stamped forms wouldn't have a job" he said with a wry smile.

After this tortuous procedure, I left to explore the city. In the centre is the magnificent Alexander Nevsky Cathedral, one of the largest Eastern Orthodox cathedrals in the world. It can accommodate 10,000 people and from the outside has the appearance of a gigantic green cake. The interior of the cross-domed basilica is decorated with exquisite mosaics and frescoes framed with ornate stonework. Disappointingly, two of the most beautiful are partly hidden by gift shops.

From the cathedral, I strolled around Bulgaria Square, an expansive esplanade in front of the National Palace of Culture. This typically Soviet-style building is the largest, multifunctional conference and exhibition centre in south-eastern Europe. In the sunshine, visitors enjoyed an outdoor photographic display and vendors sold ice cream. Here and there across the square, you could see lone men standing behind ordinary bathroom floor scales, on which people could pay to be weighed. It seemed to me little more than a slightly more dignified way of begging.

In the commercial heart of the city, towering eight metres high above the traffic and on a spot once occupied by Lenin, stands the statue of St Sofia. The figure is robed in black and the face covered in gold leaf, giving it a death-mask quality. I found out later it wasn't so popular with the locals.

That evening, my hosts invited me to join them on a trip the following day to Dupnitsa and Blagoevgrad, some forty miles south, while they attended to business. I hadn't travelled in a car for two months, so this was a novelty, and on the way home we rode high into the mountains to see the beautiful Rila Monastery, the largest and most famous Eastern Orthodox monastery in Bulgaria.

In the morning, I packed my bags and carried them down to the bottom floor to load up my bike. It seems almost dreamlike now, as I remember reaching the basement door and seeing that the padlock was missing. With some effort, I pulled on the heavy iron door and strained my eyes against the darkness, anxiously fumbling around the wall to find the light switch. In the inky blackness the switch eluded me and I tentatively reached out to feel for my bike. My heart sank and a cold numbness crept over my body as my hand fell through the air. I groped among the dust and cobwebs and this time found the switch. In the gloomy yellow light, all I could see was an empty space where my beautiful bike should be. 'I'm not thinking clearly', I told myself, 'there's bound to be an explanation', and with a knot in my stomach I climbed the stone steps of the peeling, echoing stairwell to speak to my hosts. I knocked on their apartment door and Ivo answered. "There's probably a good reason for this" I said, "but my bike's not in the basement". One look at his puzzled face told me that my worst fears were about to be confirmed. We ran down what now seemed like endless flights of steps to the ground floor. Ivo entered the basement and climbed over the dusty trestles and old broken furniture, searching the recesses of the room. With a perplexed expression, he walked outside and looked around the unkempt grassy area, one hand on the back of his head, his total bewilderment becoming ever more apparent. No doubt about it – the bike had gone.

The first thing we did was report the theft to the police. They arrived and took statements but weren't optimistic about recovery. Petya alternated between trying to reassure me and bursting into tears, especially when told the value of the bike. The police departed and my hosts left for work. As for me, I spent the afternoon curled up in bed, trying to come to terms with what had happened.

Wednesday and Thursday were black days but Ivo and Petya couldn't have done more for me. We printed posters offering a reward for the bike's return, and fixed them to walls around the block. On Ivo's suggestion, we visited flea markets to see if the bike turned up. The stalls were manned by dubious characters peddling their wares, much of which I would gladly have paid them to take away. Dogs roamed around the bustling site, as did small children leading even smaller children by the hand. We saw a few bike wrecks and one or two that looked as though their true owner might be feeling as distraught as me, but no sign of mine – or even parts of it.

In the meantime, Ivo located the main bike retailers so that I could start looking for a replacement. What else could I do? It was either that or go home. For a short while, I considered having my old road bike shipped to me from the UK but I had no idea how to go about it. I emailed Calvin at my bike shop, Ghyllside Cycles in Ambleside, for advice on transport costs and his response was immediate. "Don't even think about it," he said. "Get yourself a new bike. We have to get you back on the road. Go round the bike shops and mail me information on what's available".

Ivo and I continued to look for any sign of the stolen bike and to liaise with the police. We also visited bike shops, and in one we heard that Rohloff hubs are so rare in Bulgaria that there may be only two in the country, and that high quality bikes like mine would probably be taken to Serbia or Macedonia to be sold. Very encouraging.

The weekend approached and my hosts had to leave Sofia for a few days to visit family. Worried about leaving me on my own, Petya provided details of some events I could attend in their absence. Couchsurfing is very popular in Sofia and hosts meet regularly on a social basis, bringing along their guests if they have any. There was a meeting on the Saturday night and I went as an 'orphan' without my hosts. Around twenty people turned up, all of whom spoke English to some degree. When I related my story about the bike, they were very sympathetic, most of them feeling the need to apologise on behalf of their country.

One of the women was Mila, and during the next week, she took me to see the medieval Boyana Church to the south of the city, famous for its frescos dating back to the 11th Century. In 1979, the building was added to the UNESCO World Heritage List and had only recently been fully opened to the public. We returned to her home, and over dinner, she invited me to visit her daughter who was in an institution on the outskirts of the city, being treated for depression.

The following day, we met at the National Palace of Culture and took a series of bus rides to a village at the foot of Mt Vitosha. Mila was carrying a very heavy holdall and when I enquired, she said it contained some food for her daughter. Along the driveway of the hospital, male patients stood around staring vacantly as we passed. The grounds were overgrown and the shabby exterior of the building did nothing to impress. Inside, the stark interior was cold and the bare concrete floor echoed as we walked along the corridors. A bizarre, brightly-coloured mural adorned one wall of a staircase and at the top, a locked door with a buzzer to one side awaited. Mila pressed the buzzer repeatedly for five minutes, until finally the door opened and a nurse held it firmly ajar. A heated exchange took place between them, with the nurse insisting that the patients were sleeping and could not receive visitors. Mila was having none of it and wouldn't leave until she had seen her daughter.

After a while, Veronika emerged from the doorway looking thin and pale, and very fragile. The three of us walked down the stairs and outside into the grounds. We reached a bench where Mila opened the holdall and spread out a generous meal. Veronika answered in good English when I asked what the food in the hospital was like. "It is very nice," she said, "but there is not enough". "They don't give them nutritious food.", chipped in Mila, "That is why I bring cheese and good bread and fruit to build her up". We ate Bulgarian tomatoes (the best I have ever tasted) and solid black bread, spread with mayonnaise and dipped in sharana sol, a delicious salty mixture of spices. Two thin dogs had followed us, a mother and her pup, watching for any titbits which might come their way. Veronika was happy to feed them. "They don't get enough food either", she said, offering them pieces of bread which they devoured greedily. As we ate, a young man, another patient, walked towards us and eyed the feast. He was wrapped tightly in an overcoat, with his hands thrust into his pockets and his collar pulled up. Mila held out a sandwich and he took it eagerly. We finished our picnic and Veronika took what food she could carry. The whole experience left me thinking how lucky I was to live in the UK, with its National Health Service. Walking back to the bus stop, I questioned the lack of food. "This is what you get if you don't have money," Mila explained. "This is what the State provides."

Petya worked in the film industry, and when she and Ivo returned, we agreed it might be worth advertising the theft of the bike on the local news channel, especially as some of her colleagues had shown an interest in my trip. The Bulgarian TV crew came to film me and the interview was shown on primetime news. Sadly, it was to no avail – nothing came of it.

A follow-up visit to the police station with Ivo did nothing to raise my hopes. Our appointment was at lunchtime and police officers swaggered around the building in an informal manner, swinging bags of sandwiches from their wrists. The scene in the waiting room was almost comical. It was full of agitated characters waiting to be interviewed, and behind the far wall, sat a monumentally-bored receptionist, who was dealing with the queue of people. The only way to talk to her was through a hole in a transparent screen at the level of her face, but there were no seats on our side of the wall. This meant that enquirers were obliged to bend low to speak to her. She sat with a demoralised look on her face, while impatient men bent double to talk to her through the hatch. If they didn't bend down she ordered them to do so. I had to ask myself – why on earth wasn't there a seat on both sides?

When Ivo and I were finally granted an interview, we were shown to an untidy office piled high with dusty televisions, one of them playing away in competition with our conversation. Like his colleagues, the officer was unhelpful and arrogant, but Ivo, as usual, was politeness itself, translating for my benefit. I came away knowing I had very little chance of being reunited with my bike.

Another Saturday arrived and I concluded that there was nothing else for it but to take the plunge and buy a new bike. In the Velomania cycle shop, Dimitri a helpful young assistant, had his own tale of woe. He and two friends had all had their bikes stolen while camping in Austria. 'Now, that would be terrible', I thought – 'misery in triplicate'. The manager told me that almost every second customer had had a bike stolen, and one man had bought no less than four bikes for his son that summer. As time went on, I was to learn that Bulgaria has a reputation for bicycle theft – I wish I'd known before I arrived.

Although the shop was full of shiny new cycles, buying a touring bike, even with Calvin's help, wasn't easy. Like most nations in Eastern Europe, Bulgarians just don't tour. There was no such thing as a touring frame in the shop, all the bikes had sprung forks, and pannier racks were a big problem. Finding a front rack was the biggest challenge, yet I couldn't leave without one. After a few days, a front rack was found, and with a number of modifications, the mechanics finally succeeded in making me roadworthy.

I'd been in Sofia for three weeks by now and had become familiar with the city centre and the area in which I was staying. I was hopping on and off buses like a local and had met many wonderful people who showed me nothing but kindness and hospitality, most especially Ivo, Petya and their families. The positive side of losing the bike was that I got to know Bulgaria and its people better than any of the previous countries and their inhabitants. I'd had more interaction with people and gained a privileged insight into the Bulgarian way of life.

By the 30th of September, my new bike was ready to be collected, and it – she – had a name; quite obvious really, it was Sofi. I'd had very little exercise in the past three weeks and it was time to get my body and mind into gear for being on the road again. Sofi cost me a fraction of the price of the first bike, but I was still wary of taking her back to the apartment so Petya arranged for me to store it in her office, close to the Palace of Culture. Two days later, the three of us travelled into the city centre for the big departure. I was more nervous than when I'd left England.

With a sad goodbye to my new friends, I set off shakily in the direction of Plovdiv. It was going to take some time to get used to this new machine. Unlike the first bike, it had derailleur gears and the lighter aluminium frame meant that it handled differently. It was going to be a slow start.

The route south to Plovdiv was busy with rush-hour traffic, and as I left Sofia behind, the road surface began to deteriorate. At Vakerel, there were so many deep potholes that cars were swerving to avoid them and it was difficult to get any speed up without a constant juddering. My gear-changing skills were sadly lacking and I was becoming highly proficient at replacing the chain. In spite of my nervousness, it was a great feeling to be back on the road and I bowled along quite happily throughout the day.

Approaching Kostenets, I was corralled by three young boys on bikes who seemed to think it would be great fun to race me. They were basically bored and I was something new to distract them. They were friendly enough but still a nuisance, as it was time to find a hotel and they were slowing me down. We reached the town and intent on showing me where to stay, the boys stuck with me – I could not shake them off. In the centre, one of them stopped to speak to his mother, who reassured me that they would actually escort me to a hotel. Off we went in convoy and when another youngster tagged on, I was beginning to feel like the Pied Piper. But true to their word, they took me first to an ATM and then to an excellent hotel, homely and clean, and only twenty lev – less than ten pounds. I sent them off with a big thank you and carried Sofi up to my room without anyone noticing. No one was going to steal this baby.

The next day, I was cycling in the rain for the first time since leaving England – but I didn't care. The new bike was going well, and if anything, was more comfortable than the old one. The gel seat was certainly more rear-friendly and the butterfly handlebars were a better shape.

Four miles out of Kostenets, the rain eased but the resulting sense of enjoyment was literally brought to a halt when I had the first puncture of the trip. I wheeled over to a lay-by, removed the tyre and found a shard of glass poking through it. No worries, I had two spare tubes so I set about my first repair. This wasn't as easy as I thought and in struggling to seat the tyre rim, I managed to bend the Presta valve on the first spare. I tried with the second – same problem – I couldn't seat the tyre. The only option was to mend the puncture, but my lack of experience was becoming patently obvious. Cursing because I only had soda in my drinks bottles, lots of spitting ensued and then I pumped the tube up again and saw a hole blowing the dust on the ground. Brilliant – sticky patch applied! I'd been battling for a good hour by then, and it was starting to rain. 'Just what I need', I thought, when a car drew up and a man jumped out with his wife and daughter who spoke English. They had already passed me once on their way to the village ahead, and had recognised me from the TV appearance. Now on their way back, they could see me having problems, and the father thought he should offer to help. He seated the second spare tube, which was still in the tyre, but he had difficulty operating my hand pump. Without a word, he lifted the wheel into his car and disappeared up the road to get it inflated at the village garage. Fifteen minutes later, he returned and fitted the wheel onto the bike. I thanked them profusely and we said our goodbyes with smiles all round.

I now had two half-inflated tyres and in my ignorance, didn't know how to deflate them (boy, did I have a lot to learn!)

At the village a few miles on, I reached the garage on the main street where three young mechanics stood in the doorway. I showed them the tube I'd patched but none of them spoke English, so I mimed my request that I wanted them to deflate it so that I could pack it away. Confusion reigned when, to my alarm, they demonstrated that they wanted to pump air into it. After what was dangerously approaching a tug-of-war, one of them took the tube from me assertively and filled it with air. By then I was saying to myself, 'Well, how am I going to carry that now?', when the mechanic showed me not one but two more holes that I'd missed. Five minutes later, he returned the tube to me, patched and folded. Next, I showed them the one with the bent valve. Not a problem, they indicated and straightened the valve after checking it had no holes. I tried my best to pay them but they wouldn't take any money.

I arrived in a downpour at Pazardzhik and checked out three hotels. I was keen to get out of my wet clothes and settled on the first, a slightly faded establishment with its former grandeur still apparent. A sweeping marble staircase dominated the spacious entrance hall and I could tell that sneaking the bike upstairs wasn't going to be an option, especially as I was leaving pools of water in my wake. When I explained to the receptionist that I was worried about storing my bike because I'd had one stolen in Sofia, she also recognised me from the TV news item and couldn't do enough to help. She was more than happy for me to lock Sofi to the staircase and helped me with my bags up to my room on the second floor. She lent me an umbrella when I went out to the shop and provided me with starvestnik (newspapers) to stuff my wet shoes with on my return. What a little celebrity does for you.

The next morning, a 'Princessa' breakfast (cheese and sausage meat on toast) with two cups of '3-in-1' coffee set me up for another day's ride, now with Turkey in my sights and the feeling I got every time I left a country behind.

Plovdiv was easy to get into but a nightmare to get out of. A scarcity of route signs and street names, kept me retracing my tracks and bouncing around cobbled streets. It didn't help when a bus driver came so close to me at a set of lights, that he caught my elbow as I set off, and threw me off balance. I managed to right myself, but not without catching the back of my calf on a pedal, resulting in a nasty graze and a bruise the size of my palm.

On the way to Harmanli for my last night in Bulgaria, I veered off to a town called Haskovo to find lunch. High-rise apartment blocks covered the skyline, ugly and in bad repair and I felt sorry for the people who had to live there. No beauty to soothe their souls. I didn't stop.

Moving on, the terrain was fairly hilly but Sofi was going well and my efforts were rewarded by a two-mile downhill into Harmanli, where I spent the night.

Twenty miles of cycling the next day brought me within sight of the Turkish border and, on hearing a loud whistle on my left, I turned to see three smiling truck drivers, one of them with his arms held out towards me – it made my day.

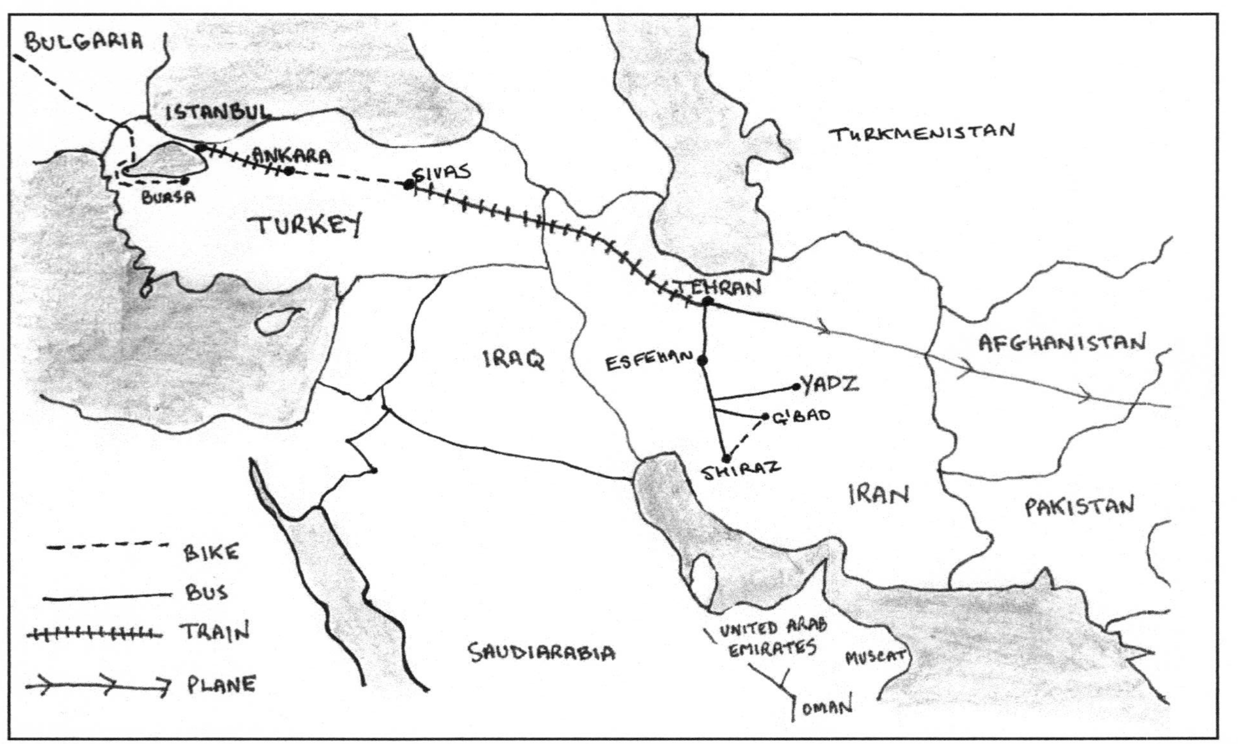
BULGARIA
ISTANBUL
ANKARA
BURSA
SIVAS
TURKEY
TURKMENISTAN
TEHRAN
AFGHANISTAN
IRAQ
ESFEHAN
YADZ
G'BAD
SHIRAZ
IRAN
PAKISTAN
BIKE
BUS
TRAIN
PLANE
SAUDIARABIA
UNITED ARAB EMIRATES
MUSCAT
OMAN

Turkey
To The Bosphorus

Getting into Turkey would have been more difficult if it hadn't been for a stroke of luck.

I approached the border with only twenty-three lev in my purse, hoping that the visa officials would take plastic. I made my way through passport control and when I got to the point of paying, the good news was that it was only £10. But that was it - 10 pounds sterling or 15 euros – nothing else was acceptable. I'd factored in having to cycle back to the nearest bank if necessary, but then I had a brainwave. I left the UK with a ten pound note in my purse and decided to hang on to it 'just in case'. In case what? – I had no idea, but there it was, at the bottom of my panniers in a spare purse. I paid my tenner and sailed across the border under a clear blue Turkish sky.

The road to Edirne was quiet and easy to follow. Even though the climate had become noticeably warmer, I ditched my shorts in favour of calf-length trousers. I was now in a Muslim country and didn't want to attract any more attention than necessary.

In Edirne, I took the cheapest hotel I could find. My room was like a shoebox, six feet long, six feet wide – just enough space for a single bed and floor space for my bags – hardly any space to stand up. On the wall above my pillow, an unnerving cast-iron radiator hung. I only hoped it stayed there.

The town was vibrant and colourful and a pleasant change from the dour provincial towns of Bulgaria. The stalls in the market were laden with fresh fruit, and pots and pans of every size and shape could be bought. In general I went unnoticed, but now and again, I was conscious of being a lone woman tourist among a majority of men. At the Pasa restaurant, I ate a meal of meat kebabs with a couple of glasses of beer and watched men having their hair cut in the barber shop next door.

A leisurely lie-in in the morning set me up before venturing out to look for breakfast. Across the road from the hotel there were three restaurants and I went into one where I was greeted by a cheery lad who spoke a little English. The conversation went like this –

“Hello, do you serve breakfast?"

“No, no breakfast. We only serve leeva."

“Oh… Do any of the other places serve breakfasts?"

“No – only leeva. All these restaurants only serve leeva."

“I see… What IS leeva?”

At that, he took me over to a wall of award certificates and showed me a news-clipping of the master chef and a plate of his 'leeva'

“Oh, liver – you only serve LIVER??"

“Yes, it's a famous dish."

‘Famous?’ I thought, ‘Really?’

“Very nice.” I said, “I like liver. I’ll come back later to try this ‘famous’ dish.”

It was hard to believe that one restaurant, never mind three in the same street, could survive only serving liver.

The rest of the day was spent wandering around the lively bazaars and visiting the fabulous Selimiye Mosque, so elegant with its four tall minarets and its vast, sumptuous, octagonal, sparkling interior. It was my first visit to a mosque and I was struck by its beauty. Quite deservedly, the Selimiye Mosque was added to UNESCO’s World Heritage List in 2011.

At midday I went back to the ‘leeva’ restaurant to try this famous meal. The bread-crumbed, deep-fried calves’ livers with salad and chilli peppers were so delicious (apart from the chillies – they were beyond me) that I returned for a second plateful in the evening.

That night I didn't get much rest. The liver overdose was keeping me awake, but it wasn't the only thing. At around 10pm, someone was hammering below my window and it continued until 12.45 when I decided enough was enough and got up to see what was going on. There, on the corner of the street, right below my window, was a man with a hammer and chisel, dressing cobble stones to repair a hole in the pavement. I started down the stairs to deal with the perpetrator and the hotel manager rushed in from the front door, promising to resolve the problem. In spite of his remonstrations, including mentioning the police, I suspected he was part and parcel of the operation. Whatever his involvement was, the hammering ceased until exactly 8am, when I was woken by it again. I packed up and departed.

Over the weeks, I kept my online journal updated and was surprised and pleased to find that not only were my family and friends reading it, but I'd developed quite a following around the world. Many readers sent messages of good will and many invited me to stay with them. One of these was teacher Kathy, who lived with her Turkish partner in Istanbul on the university campus. Istanbul wasn't on my list of places to see, because I'd heard horror stories from other cyclists, about the busy ten-lane highway leading into the city. However, Kathy knew of an alternative, quieter route from Edirne and her offer of accommodation seemed too good to refuse. Following her advice, I set off to travel south-west to Gelibolu on the north-west tip of the Sea of Marmara. From there, I would cross by ferry to Lapseki, make my way east along the south coast and catch a ferry from Bandirma to Istanbul. It sounded ideal, but what neither of us knew, was that the route was being upgraded to dual carriageway and the mix of roadworks and many unsurfaced sections would make for difficult cycling.

The landscape on the north side of the sea was one of gently rolling hills and here the roads were newly-surfaced and gleamed white, stretching endlessly into the distance. There was little to break up the monotony and the views only offered miles of dual carriageway, snaking towards a hazy blue horizon.

The heat and lack of shade were oppressive and there was nothing to distract me from the exertion, until I reached the crest of a rise and saw a stationary van with a small, loaded trailer attached. There was only one wheel on the trailer and the driver and his passenger appeared to be searching for the missing wheel in the undergrowth on the side of the road. I cycled past and forgot about it, until the van overtook me with the trailer still on its one wheel, and the opposite axle merrily bouncing along as it scraped on the tarmac. They obviously hadn't found the missing wheel.

I left the main road at a small village to look for food, passing a thin, wide, layer of grain which had been laid out on the road to dry in the sun. Along the dusty street, young children braved saying "Hello" to me and were then overcome with embarrassment when I said "Hello" back. I asked around, "Restaurant? Food?" and was directed to a butcher's shop. Not much help there. In the end, I retraced my tracks and carried on.

Uzunköprü was a different story. It was a busy town with a thriving market full of stalls laden with fresh fruit and vegetables and large bowls of sugar-coated nuts. Young men sat behind trestle tables covered in bags of loose tobacco. I asked a group of women where the Post Office was, and one of them indicated that I should follow her. Firstly, she led me zigzagging through the busy streets to her house, where she dropped off her shopping. We then carried on and the crowds became so dense that I was struggling to keep up. Seeing I was having a problem following with my bike, my guide took me by the hand to make sure we didn't get separated. When we reached the Post Office I thanked her for her kindness and she gave me a big hug. Her warmth and generosity were very touching.

Breakfasts in Turkish hotels were the best I'd had for a long time. Tomatoes, cucumber, hard-boiled eggs, olives, cheese, jam, bread and butter; yet again, a country where tomatoes are full of flavour and delicious. I've not tasted any as good in England since.

Gelibolu lies on the north side of the Dardanelles, a narrow strait linking the Sea of Marmara with the Aegean Sea. For most of the year, it is a busy tourist town, but now in low season it wasn't too packed. I caught the short ferry ride to Lapseki and was pounced upon by a perfume seller who wanted to practise his English. He gave me the full nine-yards about his personal life and an invitation to come and stay with him when I next visited Turkey – but no address.

As I cycled along on the south side of the Marmara Sea fighting a fierce headwind, I was constantly getting pips and waves from drivers of cars and trucks. Some were road workers who kept passing me as they went about their work. On one long stretch, I'd stopped halfway up a hill for a couple of minute's rest, when a truck pulled up in front of me. I was wondering what was going to happen next, when the co-driver got out waving his arms frantically, indicating that I should grab hold of the back of the truck to hitch a lift. This really amused me, because in one of Alastair Humphrey's books, he relates how drivers were always trying to shake him off from doing just this. In any case, I was fairly sure that my puny arms wouldn't take the strain of me and my loaded bike so I laughed and said, "Thanks, but no thanks".

It wasn't long before I missed a gear change and was crouched beside the bike realigning the chain. I finished cleaning my hands and a young Turkish couple on a motorbike, both dressed in full leathers, rolled up to ask me about my journey. We had a long chat and they gave me advice about ferry options to Istanbul. They were very interested in my journey and I gave them my website address before they drove off into the distance.

I reached Bandirma and started the routine search for a room. The first hotel was too expensive so I moved on and wandered up the hill. The street was lined with shops but no hotels. Halfway up the hill, a young man selling fish called to me and pointed to his stall as if I might buy something. I laughed and pointed to my bike. It was obvious I wouldn't be buying. "Fish restaurant?" he said, waving at the restaurant behind him. It all looked tempting but it was too early to eat. "Hotel?" I asked. He shouted into the shop and brought out a woman who directed me back to the bottom of the hill, reeling off a list of hotel names. With her help, it wasn't long before I found a reasonably-sized twin-room with en suite, breakfast and wifi. Happy with my find, I showered and made my way back to the fish restaurant up the hill to give them my business.

There I was 'adopted' by Harun, a deep-sea diver, and Omar, his architect colleague, both working at the nearby gas plant. They invited me to join them and plied me with food and wine. The fish was the freshest and the most delicious I'd tasted in years. It was evident from the constant chit-chat with the proprietor that they were regular customers and among the banter they told me tales of working in the area, while I told them about my trip. At the end of a convivial evening, and despite my protests, they insisted on paying the bill. As I walked back to the hotel, it was dawning on me that I would have to learn to accept generosity graciously and stop trying to be quite so independent.

In the morning I walked over to the ferry terminal to book a seat on the afternoon crossing. "Sorry," said the booking clerk, "we're on the winter schedule now, only morning and evening crossings." I was reluctant to take an evening sailing, as it was October now and the nights were drawing in. Tackling Istanbul traffic in the dark didn't appeal to me at all, so I chose the early crossing. That evening I strolled along the sea front to take in the view. The sky had turned blood red with rolling black clouds. It was incredibly beautiful but undoubtedly a portent of bad weather. I had my doubts that the ferry would sail at all the next day but just in case, I set my alarm for 6am in the morning

I dragged myself out of bed the next day, but as expected, the morning crossing had been cancelled. My options were now to take the later ferry at 18.30, or stay another night and cross the next morning. I rang Kathy to explain the situation and express my fears about cycling in the city in the dark. “That’s not a problem,” she said. “I’ll meet you at the terminal and we can cycle together.” I was much happier about this arrangement and went back to the hotel where I'd just checked out and the manager gave me back my room key.

I now had lots of time on my hands in Bandirma – time to wander round the seafront again – time to be mobbed by a gang of school kids who wanted to practise saying, "What is your name?" and then tell me theirs – time to be offered somewhere to stay by a woman who lived in nearby Bursa – and time to try the delicacies on offer for lunch, only what I had wasn’t so delicate. I ordered a ‘tost’ which turned out to be a toasted cheese sandwich with tomato sauce spread over the top. I wondered why they hadn’t put the sauce inside.

Kathy met me at the Istanbul terminal on her bike and led me through terrifying traffic, which I wouldn't have attempted to negotiate on my own.

I was made most welcome by Kathy and her partner and stayed with them for over a week, while I waited for an insurance claim form for the stolen bike to arrive in the post. My wait turned out to be in vain because the letter never did arrive, but it gave me time to visit the sights of Istanbul and arrange my Indian visa.

One of my favourite films is The Wizard of Oz and at the Indian embassy, I had a sudden feeling that I’d stepped into the scene where Dorothy reaches the Emerald City. On the 7th floor, a large panelled door was narrowly opened and a form was thrust at me. When I asked what I was to do with it, I was told through the gap to fill it in and get a letter from the British Consulate down the road. (Oh Toto …I’m never going to get to see the

Wizard! ...sob, ...sob...) At the British Consulate I was given yet another form to complete and charged sixty pounds for a letter which stated that I was actually the person shown on my passport. How crazy is that?

One thing you learn about a trip like this is that life is no longer predictable. On the way back from the Indian embassy, I was seated on the Metro when a young girl came up to me and said "Ann Wilson?" I did a double-take and uttered a "Huh – yes", thinking 'how on earth did she know my name?' "We met on the way to Bandirma", she said. "I was on the motorcycle." I was astounded. It was hard to believe that among the thousands of people in Istanbul, our paths had crossed again. Even more of a coincidence, it turned out that Karin was a student on the same Istanbul campus as I was staying.

We exchanged contact details and the following Tuesday night, I met up with her and her partner Ali, for dinner at a restaurant on the banks of the Bosphorus. The water was sparkling under the moonlight and the Blue Mosque and the Hagia Sophia were silhouetted against the skyline; together with great company and delicious food, the evening was perfect. Ali fired questions at me about my trip and I was never quite sure if he was joking when he kept telling me to make it easy for myself and catch a train. The concern of the couple for my welfare was touching. Ali was adamant that I should not cycle through the south-east of the country, in case I was imprisoned by the military. They were also worried about how I would cope with the imminent winter weather and on parting, gave me a present of fruit leather for emergency rations.

On Sunday, Kathy and I went to watch the Turkish marathon. Here we could take advantage of the only opportunity in the year to walk from Europe to Asia across the bridge over the Bosphorus. Kathy told me that the restriction was because of the past numbers of what are grimly known as 'jumpers'. After the runners have crossed, it is opened to the public for a couple of hours. Finding our way to the race wasn't easy because so many roads in the city centre were closed to traffic and we had to skirt round the route on foot. A ferry ride up the Bosphorus, followed by a bus ride, eventually took us to the Asian side of the bridge and we walked back over it, among hundreds of others, to Europe. On the European side the city was packed with people leaving the event and public transport was in a state of chaos. On Kathy's suggestion, we headed for the funicular railway, which would take us above the sea channel to an area where buses were running.

On the way, we passed the Dolmabahçe Palace and saw the guards who stand stock-still for two-hour shifts, in temperature-controlled glass boxes. I was firmly convinced they were dummies until Kathy pointed out that they sway almost imperceptibly. I'm not sure how they get out of the cases in the event of an attack but there's a guard, guarding the guards, to stop members of the public getting too close. Perhaps he lets them out.

From the funicular, we jumped onto a minibus for what seemed like a never-ending ride around the city, with the driver dodging the jams enveloping the centre.

On Monday, I visited the technical university where Kathy taught and gave a presentation to her students, showing them photos of my travels so far. Getting to the university this time by teleferik (cable car) was an interesting experience. The ride takes you 300 metres above Maçka Park and offers views over the valley behind the Dolmabahçe Palace. My presentation went well and was followed with interesting questions from the class. These came mainly from the boys, while most of the girls sat in bemused silence. I wondered if, in this male-dominated society, the girls were glad to see an independent woman showing she could manage quite well on her own.

For some time I'd been dealing with the Iranian visa agency by email and it was frustrating to say the least – the biggest problem being their slow response. Finally, I had the authorisation code and decided to travel by rail to Ankara to collect the visa on the following Monday. It was clear that I wouldn't be able to cycle the whole route in Turkey and Iran, because the winter was closing in and the distances were too great. Delays at the start of my trip and in Sofia meant that I was now behind schedule and needed to get to India in December to have the seasons back in my favour. I was hoping I would be able to cycle as far as Erzincan. There I could take a bus and avoid the worst of the weather.

On Thursday night, Kathy and I said our goodbyes over a bottle of wine and copious quantities of her homemade sage and pine liqueur. Next day, with a slightly fuzzy head, I cycled away from the campus and took a last Metro train to Taxim to collect my Indian visa from the consulate. From there I made my way to the ferry terminal to cross the Bosphorus and catch the overnight train from Yenikoy rail station on the Asian side of Turkey.

Turkey

The Trans Asia Express

This would be the first time I'd travelled by train since leaving England. Kathy had rung ahead to confirm that the bike would cause no problems, but I had my doubts. Sure enough, when I reached the ticket desk I was told emphatically that cycles were not accepted on the train. "That's not what I was told this morning", I insisted. The official was immovable and my approach was having little effect so I tried another tactic – "Well, where am I going to sleep tonight?" At this, his attitude wavered and he showed me to the station manager's office. I stood anxiously waiting, while the manager cast a cursory glance over the bike. Admittedly, laden up in all her splendour, Sofi does look a bit of a beast. "It's very small when I take the bags off", I said, hopefully. Finally, and to my relief, he gave it the nod of approval and I made my way to the train. When I got to the goods carriage, the guard demanded payment before he would accept the bike. I was sure this was unofficial but thought it best not to argue and paid up.

The traffic in Ankara is as bad, if not worse, than in Istanbul and I was thankful to get away from the main road with its underpasses and ramps, and onto the quieter University road. I would be staying with Dawn, another Couchsurfing host, and coincidentally another teacher, who lived on campus

The next day, armed with my passport, a completed application form, a wad of spare passport photos and the authorisation code from the agency, I took a bus to the Iran consulate in the heart of the city. This time the officials were very friendly and I was told I could pick up the visa the following morning.

Whilst in the consulate, I met Val and Merv from Scotland. They were also applying for visas for Iran and were cycling from England to Australia to visit family. We got on very well and went to a nearby bank to pay for the visas before having lunch together.

In the morning, I turned up at the consulate once again with Val and Merv, and we picked up our visas with no problem. For some reason, I was given thirty days but they were only given twenty-five. We didn't know why and because visas can be extended inside Iran, it didn't matter.

Another enjoyable day in their company followed, chatting over coffee and lunch and we went our separate ways at around 2pm. Val and Merv planned to catch the train from Ankara to Iran and I would set off in an easterly direction, using pedal power.

Cycling out of the city, I took the advice of Dawn, and continued on the campus road, heading south towards the city bypass. The map I had was very poor and I was rarely sure I was going the right way, but I eventually found myself on the road to Samsun, which would take me eastwards. I'd originally intended to go as far as Kirikkale, but it took longer than expected to exit the city, so I revised my goal to the nearer town of Elmadag. Turkish summertime had ended the previous weekend and it would be getting dark that much earlier.

With forty-two miles on the clock, I reached my destination at around 3pm. From a distance Elmadag was not an inspiring town. Blocks of high-rise flats painted in the most unattractive colours stood atop the hillside, blotting the skyline. I carried on to the town centre, where I was stopped by a police car and told that there were no hotels or hostels (pansions) in the town. "Yok", they said – not a thing. The chap who'd been collared to translate for the two policemen, told me I must carry on to

Kirikkale, forty kilometres further. Still hoping he would find me a room in Elmadag, I tried to look helpless and told him I'd already cycled forty-two miles and it was getting late. "Do not be afraid" he said, sounding like the Archangel Gabriel, "it is all downhill after the next big hill". 'I've heard that one before' I thought, but in spite of my protestations, there was no option but to carry on. To add to my troubles, I had to dodge three young lads intent on trying to soak me with a cup of water on the way out of town.

Well, the archangel was wrong about the distance, it was only thirty kilometres to Kirikkale, but he was more or less right about the downhill bit. It was so steep in places, I was worried my brakes would overheat – but it was a fabulous ride through stunning countryside, with fascinating rock formations and beautiful minerals on show in reds, blues, greens and yellows.

By the time I arrived at Kirikkale, it was 5pm and completely dark. I had lights on, front and back, and was wearing my reflective sash. One of the problems on entering a new town is that it's difficult to gauge when you've reached the centre. You see a hotel and a few shops and wonder to yourself, 'is this it?' I kept going in the streetlight to see if the town became more built up or thinned out and eventually stopped on a busy corner to think. The locals were hurrying home from work and while I stood amongst them wondering what to do next, a young man stopped to talk. He was very surprised to see this western woman on a laden bicycle and asked, "Where are you going? Where have you come from?" When I told him he said, "You can't stay here. There is only one hotel and it is bad. You must go to the next one ten kilometres away". I explained that this was not an option as I was too tired and it was dark. When he realised I couldn't go any further, he told me to follow his car to the hotel. I followed him through an underpass to what was the busy centre of town. On arrival at the hotel, he took me inside to translate and gave me his mobile number in case I needed any more help. And yes, it was a dump; filthy carpets and a nasty padded toilet seat.

Still, I had somewhere to stay and my bike was put in the office for safekeeping.

I didn't hang around in the morning, leaving at dawn to cover as many miles as I could in the daylight available. However, my plans were interrupted by an upset stomach which I thought I'd shaken off in Ankara. At 11.30, and only twenty-one miles down the road, I stopped at a motel restaurant for a late breakfast. My waiter was a true entertainer. He spoke no English and cheered me up no end by making animal noises to indicate what was on the menu. I asked where the next hotel was and with the help of another customer, he told me there were none before Yerkoy, sixty kilometres away. He then made an amusing sales pitch to persuade me to stay at the motel, by miming himself showering, watching TV and sleeping. By then I was laughing so much I didn't need much persuading and decided to call it a day and check in. When I'd finished eating, he led me round to the reception hall and then surprised me further, by picking up my fully-loaded bike and carrying it up two flights of stairs. I raised my arms in a 'strongman' mime, this time to his amusement.

A climb up the first hill the next day presented me with a swoop down a long, long hill and it was mostly flat going for the rest of the day to Yerkoy. I was feeling much better after ten hours sleep and covered the forty-five miles with no trouble at all. The scenery was superb – hills of browns and golds in all their hues, seen through the thin grey light of a late October sun. The weather was getting much colder and I was wearing leggings under my cycling shorts, topped off with cut-off trousers. The cotton shirt was packed away and exchanged for a long-sleeved thermal top under a fleecy jacket, plus a buff to keep the wind off my neck.

In Yerkoy, I had a few incidents with mocking teenagers, before being shown a filthy hotel by a tall, gangly, young man with long, unkempt, curly hair and a limp. I remember thinking it looked as if the place had been furnished from the local tip. He took me up four flights of bare concrete stairs to a dark, cold, dingy room and I thought I'd rather sleep in my tent than stay there. I declined the room and went back to the street, where I asked a smart, educated young man for help. He took me to a much more acceptable establishment.

In Ankara I'd been told about inexpensive places to stay in Turkey called Öğretmenevi (the ğ is silent). Officially, they are hostels for teachers, but the proprietors are flexible about guests. I knew there was one in Yozgat, only twenty-five miles away, and wanted to see what they were like, so I wasn't too concerned about the morning's slow going, caused by tricky roads, steep hills and a strong headwind.

When I reached Yozgat at 1.30, there was a wedding in full swing, and the hostel, which looked very nice, was full of wedding guests. I had the choice of pressing on another twenty miles to the next Öğretmenevi in Sorgun, or running the gauntlet of the other hotels in town. Weighing things up, I came to the conclusion that the extra mileage was probably the lesser of the two evils.

The second part of the journey was much easier than the first, but the day became colder and colder until I had to fish out my winter gloves from the depths of my panniers. The Sorgun hostel wasn't a patch on the Yozgat one, although the staff were friendly and the place had a good atmosphere. It was very cold for one thing and there was no hot water! Still, what could I expect for seven quid?

I left Sorgun at 6.30am to be sure of reaching the next town, Akdağmadeni, forty-three miles away before dark. The terrain for this stretch looked hilly on the online map and I was concerned that I might run out of daylight if it was too tough. Already my leg muscles were aching (those quads again) from the stiff going over the last four days.

The weather deteriorated as the morning wore on, and by 9 o'clock, I was feeling whacked and cold and hungry when a service station café loomed into view on the misty horizon. Ahead of me, I spotted a young man walking along the hard shoulder and it occurred to me that he was inappropriately dressed for the weather in black dress shoes and a thin white jacket which had been splattered by the spray from passing traffic.

"Hello", I said as I passed him.

"Hello – HI!," he said with that 'I'd like to talk more' tone in his voice, but I carried on. I wasn't in the mood for people practising their limited English on me. Fifty yards on I heard a cry from behind and there was the young lad running towards me gasping.

"Where are you from?"

(Oh no – here we go again...)

"England"

"What is your name?"

"What is YOUR name?" I said (I was getting impatient already.)

"Turan"

"OK – my name is Ann" I said begrudgingly.

"Ann – you are very beautiful"

"Yeah, right" (he must need glasses – I'm old enough to be his grandmother!)

"Sex?"

"Err, – I don't think so", and I pedalled off into the distance, hearing him running after me and plaintively shouting, "SEX??"

I just hoped he wouldn't follow me into the café because I really had to stop there. But no, I didn't see the poor desperate youth again. I assumed he was walking home from Sorgun after a failed night with the girls.

I had a hot bowl of soup in the café and two cups of 3-in-1 instant coffee. As the rain started to get heavier, the manager tried to persuade me to wait until it abated, but there was nowhere to stay before Akdağmadeni and I thought I ought to press on. In the toilets, I did a re-org of my clothing and ended up with six layers on top and four on the bottom, plus winter gloves. Being trussed up like that didn't make for the easiest of riding, but it did keep me warm and dry.

Thankfully, five miles before 'Akdağ' as it is known locally, I came to a long downhill which allowed me to coast all the way into the town.

I pulled up in the town centre beside a shop and my gloves were so wet that I took them off to wring them out. When I looked up, I spotted a man inside the shop laughing at me with great amusement. It was a good excuse to commandeer him for directions to the Öğretmenevi.

This Öğretmenevi was much different from the one in Sorgun, mainly because the building was as warm as toast – and for only 15TL (£6.50). I was able to have a heavenly warm shower and dry all my wet things on the hot radiators and pipes which ran around the top of the walls in my room. It wasn't long before every pipe was covered with wet laundry.

I felt I needed a day off the next day to give my legs a rest and started to seriously think about finding out about buses and trains. Looking out of my window the next morning convinced me that it should be sooner rather than later. Two inches of snow had fallen and it was still snowing. What with bad weather, steep hills, short days and a scarcity of accommodation, it was becoming unwise for me to cycle any further in Turkey. Looking at the map, I worked out that I could pick up the Trans Asia Express at the next city, Sivas, on the route Val and Merv had taken to Iran. It would be a wrench to leave the snug, cheap hostel, but organising the train might need more than one personal appearance at the station, so I should give myself plenty of time. I hopped on a bus that afternoon.

The Öğretmenevi I found in Sivas was more of a hotel and cost three times as much, but I did get breakfast and it was a little more comfortable, if not quite as cosy as the one in Akdağ. At the station, I was told that the Trans Asia Express only leaves on a Thursday. Today was Tuesday, and hanging around would seem to be a bit of a waste of time and money, but my stomach still wasn't right and I needed to be close to a toilet (probably from being so variably hot and cold). Being stuck on a train right now probably wasn't the best idea anyway, and perhaps my insides would settle down by Thursday. I couldn't buy a ticket until the day of departure and even though I didn't get a negative response about the bike, I still expected to have the same battle on my hands as I had had in Istanbul. The best thing would be to give myself a few hours on the day to haggle with the guards and the station manager. Goodness only knows what I'd do if they didn't give way this time.

My days in Sivas were mainly spent thumb-twiddling. It was too cold to go anywhere, apart from a few sorties for food and to fill my wallet with enough euros to last me all my time in Iran. The ATMs there only accept Iranian bank cards, and every source told me to take all the cash I was going to need with me. I also bought a long top and a scarf so I could comply with the Iranian dress laws for women.

Thursday came and I stayed in the hotel until lunchtime to minimise my waiting time at the station. At 2pm, I was at the ticket desk and asked for a single to Tehran, to include a bike. Apart from it taking nearly two hours to book Sofi in, the process went without a hitch. Numerous phone calls were made and endless forms were filled in. The porters even weighed the bike and all the time I was thinking 'It's only a flippin' bike for goodness sake!', but everyone was friendly and cheerful and I was relieved that there was no opposition to contend with. For some reason, the train was scheduled to leave at 10pm and not 18.40 as stated on my first enquiry, so I left Sofi in the luggage area, happy she was secure and walked back into town. With nothing much to do, I returned to the Öğretmenevi and explained my situation, asking if I could sit in the lounge for a while. The staff were more than helpful and even gave me a ticket for a free cup of tea.

I was back at the station at 8pm and a young man in snappy clothes and disturbingly white patent leather shoes approached me. He spoke no English, but insisted on talking to me. I became a little suspicious of his perseverance after a while, and when he started making suggestive actions, I came to the conclusion he was a male prostitute. I left him and went to check on Sofi. She was still where I'd left her in the luggage area and the station staff invited me into their brew room for a coffee. Two of the porters were deaf mutes and one of them offered me a slice of some kind of pear. It was extremely sour and I couldn't hide my distaste. When he wrote down that he was deaf, I made him look at my screwed up face and everyone laughed. In spite of his disability, he understood some English and we ended up communicating quite well, even exchanging email addresses. In fact, I had a longer conversation with him than I'd had with many a hearing/

speaking Turk. True to form, the train didn't arrive until after eleven, by which time I was shattered and struggling to keep warm. Nonetheless, I was still excited to be on the way to Iran, starting a new part of my journey.

As I climbed on the train with all my panniers, a woman from the next carriage beckoned me forcefully to follow her. She was an Iranian with a strong-boned face and deep set eyes. "This is my carriage" I said, looking at the number on my ticket and turning the opposite way. "Not use numbers" she said and waved me towards her. "I will look first" I replied, but as she said, the compartment I should have been in was full. I squeezed back along the corridor with my bags and was stopped again by the woman. "You can share with me or there is an empty compartment further down". I was far too tired to make conversation and took the empty compartment. I settled down in a fairly comfortable bunk and had no trouble crashing out until morning.

The next day, I watched the Turkish scenery pass by in bright sunshine and wished I was cycling. The woman, whose name was Mina, had assumed ownership of my welfare for some reason, and called me into her compartment to talk to her as she cracked walnuts in her hands and shared them. Mina was in her thirties, but wasn't married and lived with her mother near Tabriz. She was wearing a casual top and trousers and I asked why she didn't have her head covered. "No need yet", she said and then showed me her passport photo, in which she was wearing a traditional black veil or *maghnae* covering her hair and a black coat or *manteau*. Her face was quite beautiful and the heavy eye make-up in the photo enhanced it even more. As she spoke, her manner seemed abrupt and bossy but she understood my reaction and apologised, explaining it was the Iranian way. Her strong personality was a little overwhelming and I had to extricate myself from her company to find a little peace in the restaurant carriage. I'd eaten my own food for breakfast but was now ready for a hot meal and the chicken kebab with rice and salad was very good.

The train arrived in Tatvan on the western edge of Lake Van at 10pm. In the dark, we gathered our belongings and boarded a ferry for the town of Van, four hours away. By then it was pitch black and I saw nothing of Lake Van, so the time was spent observing the other passengers and changing a few euros for riels. A sign attached to a wall by the stairs amused me; instead of the usual 'No Entry' it said, 'UPPER DECK - TO SAVE YOUR LIFE DO NOT GO UPSTAIRS". What was up there? – A kraken?

We boarded another train in Van and Mina hurried me along to share a carriage with her. I bedded myself down and slept until 4am when the train came to a halt. Instructions in Turkish and Iranian were being announced by guards in the corridor and Mina ushered me off the train. We had reached the Turkish/Iranian border at Kapikoy and all passengers disembarked to go through passport checks on the Turkish side. This took a good hour and I'd jumped off the train with only sandals on my feet. The train was locked and we were not allowed back on, until everyone was checked, so my toes froze! There were still more passport and ticket checks between Kapikoy and Tabriz, so sleep was grabbed in thirty minute chunks.

Iran

Fulfilled Expectations

Morning came and we were now into our third day. The food on the Iranian side of the border was not good. Breakfast consisted of sheets of bread resembling cardboard, with butter and honey, and lukewarm coffee.

Around midday, we reached Tabriz and everyone disembarked again, this time for luggage checks. Until now, only a few women had worn head coverings but here we all covered up. On the platform alongside the baggage van, luggage was distributed to the owners and every case was opened for inspection. Clothes and gifts spilled onto the platform. I stood watching the porters handing down bags, and after the last one was grabbed, I asked where my bike was. "No blue bike – just this silver one", said the guard. Panic waved over me and I had visions of joining that number of rare cyclists who have had multiple bikes stolen. While I was wringing my hands, the other passengers watched the proceedings with bated breath. Five minutes later, one of the porters wheeled out dear Sofi (the bike is inscribed with 'Drag' which I found later means 'Dear' in Bulgarian). What a relief! I almost felt guilty she'd had to ride in the luggage van.

I'd noticed along the journey, that whenever Mina and I disembarked, she seemed to know many of the male passengers and rail staff. I didn't think too much of it until we climbed back on the train and a man in his fifties sidled into our carriage, closing the door behind him and drawing the curtains. Mina introduced us and then got up and locked the carriage door. They were obviously very good friends and gazed into each other's eyes as they held hands and had an intimate conversation, which turned into nothing less than a canoodling session. I'd have put money on him having a wife further up the train. This put me in a rather difficult position. I would have preferred to leave them to it and go to the dining car, but the door had been locked and I could tell I was expected to stay. I buried my head in a book until he left. As I waited, I turned the events over in my head and wondered exactly why Mina was on the train. Did she have some other motive and had she collared me to give her an air of respectability? The visitor finally left and I took my chance to escape for a cup of tea.

Evening came and Mina explained that the restaurant was now closed. Our next meal would be brought to us, and I had to choose what I wanted for dinner. I wasn't quite sure how this would work out but I chose fish. What arrived was not the gourmet surprise I might have hoped for. Dinner was in a brown paper bag and consisted of more strips of cardboard bread, a rusted tin of tuna and a carton of apple juice. The tuna had the consistency and taste of something that had been in a can for twenty years. I left the food and drank the juice.

At 3am, after more hours of broken sleep, we arrived in Tehran and proceeded to the baggage reclaim area of the sleepy station. Mina had left the train and I was once again on my own. My plan was to somehow get to Esfahan, but I had no idea how and arriving in the capital at this hour wasn't going to make things easy. While waiting for Sofi to appear on the carousel, I got chatting to the daughter of a family who lived in Esfahan and she invited me to travel with them by coach. Before I knew it, Sofi was bungeed into the boot of a saloon taxi, and by 4.15am, I was on a bus for a seven hour ride, arriving at Esfahan just before noon.

Two nights of very little sleep didn't do much for my powers of investigation, and after cycling a couple of miles into the city centre, I checked into the first hotel I saw. I unpacked my panniers with the idea of crashing out immediately, but then thought I should check my mail. To my delight, an email from Val and Merv informed me that they were also in Esfahan, on the other side of the city. The wi-fi connection died before I could respond but I was so excited, I forgot how tired I was and set off on my bike to find them.

What a thrill it was to meet up again. In the centre of the city we walked through the exquisitely beautiful Imam Square, with its mosques and palace, and along the banks of the Zayande River, passing the thirty-three arches of the Si-o-seh Bridge illuminated stunningly against the night sky. We exchanged stories about our train journeys and stopped for a freshly-pulped carrot drink before returning to our respective hotels. My friends left two days later for Shiraz, and we once again promised to keep in touch. I would later follow them, but firstly I wanted to see more of this magnificent city and its wonders.

My impressions of the country were mixed. Many Iranians were welcoming and some invited me to stay in their homes. Most people couldn't do enough to help, to the point of being overwhelming. However, Iran sees relatively few westerners, and men of all ages, stared and said 'Hello', with no intention of holding a conversation. Western women were obviously a curiosity and I was advised not to stare back as it would be misinterpreted as a 'come-on'. At first I found it annoying to be the target of these quips and not be able to give a riposte, but I did find a way to respond. When young men shouted a cheeky, "Hello", I'd occasionally take delight in stopping and politely asking them for directions. They clearly didn't expect to have to actually talk to me, and more often than not it left them embarrassed and struggling for words. A few genuinely did want to talk and were happy to engage in conversation, usually showing concern about the impression the outside world has of their country – that was if they weren't trying to sell me a carpet.

In ancient times, Esfahan was a vital stop along the Silk Road and the Imam Square was a busy arena of entertainment and business, exchanged between people from all corners of the world. The central open area covers almost 1000 square feet and is bordered by the Ali Qapu Palace, the Lotfolla Mosque and the Shah Mosque. The fourth side is bounded by the Imperial Bazaar, an historical market and one of the oldest and largest bazaars in the Middle East. I spent hours strolling around the exquisite, blue-tiled buildings, admiring the high archways, minarets and domes and taking delight in the wares in the bazaar. In a park on the banks of the river, I was passed by the first young Iranian women I'd seen on bicycles. I was told later that it is forbidden in Iran for women to ride bikes, so they were taking a risk.

Food was proving to be a little monotonous. There were a few burger bars, but most restaurants were limited to kebabs and rice. I ate Obergon stew, which I think was goat, and decided it tasted better than it looked. Very little English was spoken and on entering a street café close to the Imam Square, the young male staff were so terrified of having to speak to me that I gave up and left. It was obviously going to be a challenge travelling through this country on my own.

Most of Thursday morning was spent with travel agents, tourist assistants and money exchangers, and by lunchtime, I had booked an onward flight to India, a bus ride to Shiraz and a hotel. While hunting for the travel agent, I fell into conversation with a teacher who helped me with directions. He told me that life in Iran was so restricted that people had little more to do than work and stay at home. Rules regarding interaction between men and women meant that family leisure activities such as sports and dining out were non-existent. Complaints about the government were to become a constant theme as I travelled in this country.

In the afternoon I crossed the Si-o-seh Bridge on my way to Vank Cathedral in the Armenian Quarter, passing numerous women wrapped in voluminous black veils or chadors. Inside the cathedrals, the frescoes depicting heaven and hell were striking in their gory colourfulness and the style of some of them rather humorously resembled cartoons. I was careful not to laugh. In the adjoining museum, a remarkable exhibit caught my eye; a prayer written on a human hair, which could be viewed through a magnifying glass.

I walked back towards the bridge and stopped at a stylish street café behind the cathedral where I had the best cappuccino I'd had in months. As I sat listening to familiar lounge music and admiring a print of Hopper's 'Nighthawks' above the counter, a polite young man asked if he could join me. We chatted for some time and the conversation once again turned to how unhappy he was with the restrictions of life in Iran. He worked in information technology, but was subject to constant supervision by the government and was very dissatisfied with his job. His real ambition was to be an artist, but he couldn't make a living that way.

When the day came for me to move on to Shiraz, I cycled to the bus station where I loaded Sofi and the panniers into the luggage compartment of the bus and went to a kiosk to buy a drink for the journey. There was a young lad behind the counter and he was chatting with another male youth. They both looked bemused as I approached, but I was getting used to this sort of thing, so I didn't take much notice. After some heavy going, involving asking for a coke and getting an orange drink, I paid up. The two lads were still looking at me and smirking to each other and I was getting annoyed.. "Where are you from?" said the one behind the counter with a grin. "England" I said. "You don't see many English people do you?", I sarcastically followed up with – knowing full well that they wouldn't understand me. I returned to the bus feeling irritated by them. When I sat down I understood the source of their amusement – I still had my helmet on – on top of my scarf....

The journey took over eight hours instead of the scheduled six and I arrived in Shiraz in the dark. Luckily, with only a basic map of the city and a few directions from helpful passers-by, I located my hotel fairly quickly and checked in. In the reception area, a group of men were gathered. They invited me to join them and the evening was spent drinking coffee and listening to their political views. Once again, the talk centred on their opposition to the government and its restrictive regime, and I heard horror stories of opponents to the recent election result having been tortured and raped. Later in the evening, we were joined by a holy man in black turban and gown, who I was told agreed with them. Surprisingly, at the suggestion of the group, I took photos of us all, including the holy man. The whole situation seemed a little surreal, and I wondered later if I had been part of a set-up to spread the word to the West.

Dominating the centre of Shiraz is the Citadel of Karim Khan, with its southeast tower leaning at a steep angle from the cracked citadel wall, as a result of subsidence into the sewerage system. I walked round the perimeter and wandered into the Vakil Bazaar, where the aroma of colourful spices and dried herbs filled the air. Bags of nuts and seeds covered shelves in the kiosks and beautiful Persian carpets hung from rails. Bales of vivid, glittering material were piled high on stalls, and women in their black chadors searched through them, making their choice. I wondered when they would wear such bright garments.

In the afternoon, I walked to the tourist information office on the outskirts of town and then caught a bus back. The gender discrimination that forces women to sit at the back of buses was a new and unpleasant experience. Apart from the indignity, it's a highly inefficient system. Women mount the steps at the front of the bus to buy a ticket, and must then climb down to walk to the back entrance. Nonetheless, I wasn't about to argue.

That night I walked through the warren of streets looking for bread and passed a chador-swathed woman with a stack of lavash, or unleavened flatbread, draped over her arm. When I asked her where the bakery was, she lifted one of the flat loaves and gave it to me, refusing any payment. The culture of sisterhood among women was apparent and touching – perhaps even a necessity.

Iran

"I Am Not a Terrorist!"

In spite of the underlying political turmoil within the country, I was determined to cycle at least some of it. I had a route in mind from Shiraz to Yazd which, with a short detour, would take me past the ancient city of Persepolis. It was a six-day ride in a north-easterly direction, and would involve two nights of wild camping. I have to admit, it did fill me with some trepidation. My intention as always, was to keep to my plan unless events persuaded me to opt out. I expected these events to be either suffering from cold, or feeling vulnerable.

The first day worked out well. I'd been out of the saddle for two weeks and thirty-three miles of riding to Persepolis was enough get the old legs working again. The scenery was spectacular. In the distance, craggy mountains rose in different shades of brown and grey under a cloudless blue sky. Shepherds, with their heads wrapped in scarves, drove herds of sheep and goats on the sandy terrain. Against the hazy background of the mountains, they presented a biblical scene. Cars and trucks honked their horns and some even slowed down to take a photograph or video me on their phones. As I cycled through the town of Marvdasht, I drew lots of attention from the locals. Two boys passed me on a scooter and the driver looked back at me and guffawed loudly. My hackles were up and I copied his guffaw back. He laughed again and I copied him again. I know it was childish, but it gave me a smidgeon of satisfaction as he disappeared among the traffic ahead. Arriving at Persepolis, I rejected the first hotel on the approach to the ruins on the basis of price. I was glad I had, because the second one was closer to the historic site and 10,000 Rials – 60p cheaper – a much better deal.

In the early afternoon, I met three cyclists who were leaving for Shiraz. They were cycling my intended route in reverse and were full of useful information. Their previous night had been spent in a mosque in a small town fifty miles away. Prior to this, the road had ascended to an altitude of almost 8,000 feet. They'd camped one night in a builder's yard which had been very cold – not encouraging. However, because of the time of year, the desert stretch was not too hot – some good news. I decided to carry on to the mosque and reassess. I could always turn back.

While we talked, two Americans with their Iranian guide joined us. They were full of admiration for our tenacity in cycling in Iran, the guide especially so. "We passed a woman cycling on her own earlier", he exclaimed, "on our way from Shiraz!" "That was probably me", I said. I'd changed out of my cycling clothes by then and the guide was amazed to discover that indeed I was the lone woman cyclist he'd passed earlier.

I spent the next day wandering around the ruins of Persepolis and soaking up the atmosphere of this fabulous historic site. To see the columns and reliefs in situ, the like of which I had only ever seen in books and museums, was a truly moving experience. It was easy to imagine the inhabitants moving about the buildings and hallways in ancient times. In all the time I was there, I saw only a handful of visitors and felt immensely privileged.

With one last look at the ruins, I set out the next day on the old road heading north. It was relatively quiet and gave some respite from the traffic until I re-joined the main road. Again, the mountainous scenery was eye-wateringly beautiful.

At Sivand I stopped briefly to buy food and then moved on to Sa'adat Shar, where I again caused quite a stir among the men. At the far end of town, I was relieved to find a quiet grassy area to sit and grab a bite to eat. Even there, I was spotted by the odd motorcyclist who came to check me out. One young chap asked me where I was from and if I was travelling alone. In the circumstances I thought it prudent to say 'No' and gestured that I was following my companions.

All of this attention was nothing compared to my reception in the next small town. I'd covered fifty-five miles by the time I reached the outskirts of Garderabad, which I could see below me from the road. The pipping and shouting from vehicles was becoming a little wearing and I hoped that like the cyclists I'd met at Persepolis, I could find shelter in the mosque to get away from it. When I arrived in the centre, the main street came to a standstill as everyone stopped to watch me. A horde of young boys, riding small motorbikes and bicycles in pairs, circled round and followed me, shouting and waving with glee. Groups of men stood with smiles on their faces and hands in pockets, enjoying the disturbance. It was as if the circus had come to town. The commotion continued as I searched up and down the street for the mosque. It had been visible from the main road but was now out of sight. Becoming more and more agitated, I came to a halt in front of half a dozen men who stood enjoying the entertainment. "Does anyone speak English?" I demanded. One surprised chap was pushed forward by the others and he directed two boys on a motorbike to lead me to the mosque, which they obediently did.

I rolled up at the gate and found it locked. While I was wondering what to do next, a car drew up beside me. The driver was a handsome young man who spoke a little English and offered to help. My patience was wearing thin by now, but I explained politely that I was seeking shelter in the mosque because I had nowhere to stay and wanted to talk to the holy man. What followed was a conversation of misunderstandings;

"You cannot stay here. You must stay at my house", said the young man. I was in no mood to be sociable by now and said,

"Thank you but I'd rather stay in the mosque."

"The mosque is not a good idea", said the young man.

"Do you have a wife and children?" I asked

"No."

"You live alone?"

"Yes."

"In that case I couldn't possibly stay with you."

"I am a very good man", he said, looking affronted, "A very, *very* good man!"

"And I am a woman alone. I cannot possibly stay with you."

Quite amusingly, he said, "I am not a terrorist – get in the car!"

To which I replied, "Certainly not!"

He finally relented and begrudgingly took me inside the mosque to meet the holy man, who wasn't at all keen on me staying there. Whether it was because I was a woman alone, or because he could see that I had another offer, I don't know, but he enthusiastically vouched for the young man's integrity, who, in actual fact, was inviting me to stay in his parent's home. Next thing, I found myself talking on the young man's mobile to Malek, a fluent English speaker, who appeared five minutes later to translate and vouch for the young man. By now it was getting late, and I needed to make a decision. It appeared I was about to experience the Iranian hospitality I had heard about and as my options were diminishing, I accepted. I was bundled into a car with my bags, and one of the young boys still in attendance was instructed to follow behind us on Sofi.

My mind was whirling as I entered Amahl's house. His mother was totally unfazed by my appearance and greeted me as if it was the most normal thing in the world to receive a lone English woman as a guest. The large reception room was bare of furniture and the floor was covered in exotic Persian carpets and bolsters. I was invited to sit down and his mother brought me a tray of tea, golden and mild. She instinctively knew that I might find sitting on the floor a problem and offered me a plastic chair. I felt awkward perched up there looking down on everyone and it wasn't long before I ended up on the floor, where Amahl's sisters banked me up with brightly-covered cushions, whenever they saw me sliding. Soon more relatives arrived, eager to have their photos taken with the foreign visitor.

When evening came, Malek arrived and a feast was laid before us, prepared by Amahl's mother and his sisters; chicken, rice, pasta, bread, salad, yogurt and some tasty leaves. Large jugs of *doogh*, a yogurt drink similar to Turkish *ayran*, accompanied the food. The women of the family withdrew to another room and Amahl's younger brother joined us. As we ate, the four of us discussed Iran and England and the many differences in our lifestyles. It was difficult for the men to comprehend my journey, but they listened as I told them where I had been and where I planned to go. They explained some of their country's customs and I learned a few disconcerting facts. As well as cycling being illegal for Iranian women, it is against the Muslim religion for women to sing. Also, no woman would live alone for fear of being attacked. The subject of my next stop at Safa Shahr came up in the conversation and there was great concern that I was considering camping wild. "It is not safe", said Amahl, offering to drive me to the next hotel at Surmaq. I said my only worry was about the cold and they confirmed that it would be very cold at that height. I tossed over the pros and cons in my head and reluctantly agreed to accept a lift.

I slept on blankets on the floor and in the morning, breakfast was brought to me on a tray laden with bread, honey, chocolate spread, rich cream and cheese, all accompanied by tea served with *nabat,* huge yellow rocks of sugar crystals. After the meal, Amahl took me for a tour of the local sights. We drove to Pasargadae, to see the tomb of Cyrus the Great, the founder of the

Persian Empire, and on the way back stopped off at a bakery where naan bread was being made.

By mid-afternoon, we were ready to leave for Surmaq, with Sofi bungeed in the back of the family pickup truck. Outside, I asked Amahl's mother to pose for a photograph but she was having none of it and wouldn't be taken as she was. She disappeared into the house and I expected her to reappear with her apron removed and her hair combed. I was stunned when she came out covered from head to foot in a brilliant turquoise dress and matching veil, sewn with sparkling sequins. Now I could see what the fabulous material in the Shiraz bazaar was for.

I said my goodbyes to the women and Amahl drove me the seventy miles to Surmaq. At the 'Touristy' hotel I had my second unpleasant experience of the gender division in Iran. It was a cold, dismal place, devoid of guests and I wasn't reassured when the manager entered the dark reception area to the sound of his echoing footsteps. "Do you speak English?" I asked – my usual initial enquiry. I could have been forgiven for thinking I'd suddenly become invisible when he looked straight through me and turned to Amahl who had followed me in. Amahl was obviously embarrassed, and spoke to the manager in Farsi to ask about a room for me. It may have been unreasonable of me, but my feathers were ruffled. Until now, any Iranian man I had spoken to was forced to respond because I was alone. I didn't like the atmosphere in this place. It was unfriendly and I didn't want to stay there by myself. "Let's try the next hotel", I said. When we arrived at Abadeh, the hotel there was very different. A polite manager was happy to speak to me and the room was fine.

I said a sad goodbye to Amahl and, alone in my room, I turned over the events of the previous day when I'd been treated like a queen. I'd revelled in the company of Amahl and his family, and now, for the first time since setting off, I felt quite desolate.

I knew that Abadeh was on the main bus route and as I was having misgivings about being a lone woman cyclist in Iran, I made some enquiries and the next day caught the bus to Yazd. In hindsight, I think I was far too cautious and I now wish I had cycled across the desert.

Yazd had to be my favourite city in Iran, possibly because it's smaller and quieter than either Esfahan or Shiraz. Close to the Jameh mosque are two hotels, the Silk Road and the Orient, both under the same ownership. They cater specifically for foreigners and it's easy to find English speakers. Each has its own charm, and the internet at the Orient where I stayed, is shared by residents of both. I could meet people in the 'coffeenet' at my hotel, or go over to the Silk Road for a pot of tea and chat with the other travellers. There I tried camel curry for the first time, and it was very good.

In the evenings, I was so glad I was staying in the Orient. To watch a sunset from its rooftop is an unparalleled experience. As the sun goes down, the clear sky turns to a deep azure blue, with golds and pinks glowing above the outline of the rooftops on the horizon. From the minarets of the mosques, vivid sapphire lights reflect on the golden domes and produce a paint-pot of colours – a memorable sight.

One evening, I was with Camilla and Alexandra, two guests at the Silk Road, exploring the maze of alleyways of the old town which were lined with walls of adobe and straw. Down a narrow street, we moved into single file to allow a motorbike to pass. The two of us at the back watched in horror as the driver reached out and grabbed Camilla's rear and then sped on. We were all quite flabbergasted (especially the girl who's bum was pinched!) but then heard the motorbike turn round and head back towards us. "Right girls", I said, "let's block him!" The driver's face was a picture as we formed a wall and forced him to stop. Alexandra, who speaks Farsi, told him sternly that he was 'very rude', while I gave him a good thump on the back.

Feeling fairly well satisfied, we walked on and discovered why he'd turned round – it was a dead end.

I spent five nights in Yazd, and during that time Amahl and I kept in contact by mobile phone. Later in the week, he was coming to Yazd to see his sister at the University and asked if I would like to return with him to stay with his family again. I gladly agreed.

He arrived on the Monday in his friend Assad's car. The size of the vehicle had me wondering if I should catch the bus, but they had other ideas. "Take apart", said Amahl, and, after some persuasion I agreed to dismantle the bike. I expected them to put it in the back, but then I didn't know that we were picking up his friend's wife on the way back. This meant that the bike had to go in the front passenger seat – well, nothing was too good for Sofi. I wouldn't have thought it was possible to get a bike, four panniers and four adults into a Peugeot 206, but it can be done.

Before leaving Yazd we stopped off to see the Zoroastrian Atash Behram temple which enshrines the 'Victorious Fire'. The sacred flame is alleged to have been burning since 470 AD and sits within an amber-tinted glass enclosure. Only Zoroastrians are allowed to enter the sanctum area. We had to view it through the glass.

We drove back to Amahl's house and I spent two more wonderful days being spoiled again by his family. The bike was already half dismantled so we finished the job and packed it into a large cardboard box, ready for the overnight bus journey to Tehran airport.

Something I couldn't understand was why Amahl kept calling me 'Wilson'. He was intelligent and spoke enough English to know my name. One day I challenged him and he said he couldn't possibly call me Ann, so I concluded it must be a taboo word in Persian. All was explained after I returned home and did some digging – *ann* is the Persian word for – 'shit'. If I ever return to that part of the world, it might be an idea to use another name.

On the last day, a special meal was cooked for me. It was interesting to see how different the preparation was from European methods. One of the daughters sat on the floor holding the meat high, while her mother cut small pieces from it and dropped them into a bowl. This was to make *abgoosht*, a lamb stew with the meat served in one bowl and the 'soup' in another. Bread is torn up and eaten with the liquid and the stewed meat is eaten separately. In the evening, other members of the family arrived, making ten of us seated on the floor. It was a delicious meal and a lovely evening – a fitting end to my stay.

On the last day, Amahl and I visited Malek and we sat around eating a traditional snack of walnuts and senjeds, a fruit not unlike a small date. Malek would have liked me to stay and dine with his family but my overnight coach seat was booked and I would soon be leaving.

Back at Amahl's house, I said goodbye to his parents and was about to hug his sisters but they insisted on coming with us. Night fell as we drove to a layby on the main road, and it was a surprise to see Malek pull up in his car. It was going to be a sad farewell for everyone. The sleeper coach arrived and there was the usual haggle about the cost of my boxed bike. This time it was between Amahl and the driver and I understood not a word. The price was finally agreed and Amahl paid. There was no question of my reimbursing him; it would only have given offence. The last parting as I boarded was even more emotional than the first. We had become firm friends and I left feeling that I must return. Iran had fulfilled all my expectations.

After breakfast at the Hotel Hafez in Tehran, I met a European woman who was working in Qatar and had come to Iran for a holiday. She was an overbearing person and expounded on how relaxed Iran was compared to Qatar. When I asked about Qatar, she went into detail about the extreme heat there and the restrictions on women, who had to be completely covered in burkas. The conversation was held in front of an Iranian receptionist dressed in her hijab. She understood English and I felt it was the wrong message for her to be hearing, given the dress restrictions on Iranian women. I changed the subject and mentioned that I'd been cycling for many miles and was about to cross India. The bossy European told me it would be impossible. "You can't cycle in India!" she declared. "The roads are full of bicycles, animals and vehicles. It's MUCH too dangerous!" "Hmmm," I thought, "we'll have to see about that."

Pushing over the Swiss Alps

Serbian bus stop

Waiting for the Trans Asia Express

Cycling dress, Iran

Ivo and Petya, Sofia, Bulgaria

Persepolis, Iran

Part Two

The Saga of a Sickly Cyclist

LAHORE
AMRITSAR
CHINA
PAKISTAN
CHANDIGARH
TIBET
NEW DELHI
NEPAL
JAIPUR
BHUTAN
LUCKNOW
BIHAR
ALLAHABAD
BANGLADESH
JHARKHAND
AHMEDABAD
INDIA
WEST BENGAL
SURAT
KOLKATA
MUMBAI
HYDERABAD
BAY OF BENGAL
PLANE
GOA
BIKE
CHENNAI
KOCHI

India

The Border Ceremony

The flight from Tehran was uneventful until we came within reach of Amritsar. As usual, the pilot's voice came over the tannoy, informing us we would soon be descending and should fasten our seat belts. The flight attendants took their seats. All was well until the second we felt the plane begin to descend and a number of Indian men left their seats, opened the overhead cabin storage and started to take their hand luggage out. Complete mayhem had broken out. The young flight attendants jumped up in horror and ordered everyone to return to their seats until the seatbelt signs were switched off. The miscreants begrudgingly did as they were told, and apart from the impending danger they caused, it was difficult not to find the whole incident hilarious.

I arrived in the city late at night and rang a guide-book-recommended hotel from the airport. As I expected, the taxi driver tried to take my business elsewhere, telling me that the hotel I was heading for was "costly". That may have been so, but it was the middle of the night and I wasn't willing to be taken to an unknown destination after arriving in a new country.

I was dropped off at The Grand Hotel and could see the staff through a window, sleeping on the floor in the reception hall. A few good bangs on the door roused them and I was checked into a room with no questions asked about the very large parcel that accompanied me.

My first Indian breakfast was a paper-thin omelette, sweet white toast and black tea; a fairly familiar meal for a change. At the reception desk I perused leaflets advertising excursions in the city and booked myself on a trip to see the India/Pakistan border ceremony that evening. Venturing onto the street to see what life in India looked like, I saw that the description by the woman in Tehran was reasonably accurate. Dusty streets teemed with every kind of transport: bicycles, motorbikes, cycle rickshaws, motorised rickshaws, horse driven carts, buses and cars, all jostling for space. However, apart from the odd stray dog, there were few animals, but it wasn't only the sight of the melee which assaulted my senses, it was the noise. Everything with a horn was blowing it, giving the scene an impression of complete chaos. Buildings were emblazoned with brightly-coloured advertising signs in English and Hindi but there was no evidence of decorative or structural maintenance. Electric cables were strung like washing lines from building to building and wrapped around telegraph poles, with no discernible semblance of order. Roads and pavements were littered with the rubbish of ages. For me to attempt to join the throng on a bicycle seemed like total madness. I just hoped it would be less hectic outside the city.

Anyway, that problem was for another day – I was going to spend a few nights here to acclimatise myself. My first objective was to find a map, and as luck would have it, my hotel was close to a tourist information office. The service I received made me realise that I would have to manage my expectations in this new land. The girl assistant was very polite but unable to provide me with a street map of the city or any printed information on local sights:

"We don't have any maps," she said, "but I will tell you how to get to the Hall Bazaar, where you can buy one."

"But I need a map to get there."

"No, no, I will give you directions."

"I won't remember them. You're a tourist office, why don't you have a map of the town – or any information leaflets?"

"You don't need a map. I can tell you everything you need to know. We have visitors coming in here with their guide book and after I have given them all the information they want, they put their book away and don't use it again".

I could see I was getting nowhere. "You will have to write everything down for me", I insisted, "and draw me a map." She could tell I wasn't convinced by her method and downloaded a very basic town plan from her computer. I left feeling a little less than satisfied and went back to the hotel to recover from the jet lag.

At 3pm, I left the hotel in a taxi shared with a young Swiss couple, Romy and Christian. We were heading northwest of the city to the border ceremony and calling at a small temple on the way. Removing our shoes and socks at the temple was mandatory and we walked across a busy road in bare feet. The ground was less than clean and I hoped I wouldn't pick up something undesirable as I stepped among the dirt and dust. Inside the temple, we threaded our way through gaudy shrines, waterfalls and mirrored walls, so different from anything I'd seen before.

The road leading to the border was lined with stalls selling food and crowds of people threading their way between vehicles to see the ceremony. There is only one border crossing between Pakistan and India and it traverses the Grand Trunk Road at Wagah, northwest of Amritsar and southeast of Lahore. The daily 'retreat' ceremony is intended to be a way of ending hostilities for the day and the soldiers take it very seriously. The Indian border guards are dressed in brown military uniforms with elaborate red and gold cockscomb headdresses to accentuate their strutting march. This is meant to imitate the pride and anger of a cockerel, but for the majority of the audience, the activities raised many laughs. There were thousands of Indians and a few foreign tourists seated on 'our' side, and only a handful of Pakistanis on the opposite side of the strong dividing gate. The atmosphere was like a football match, with everyone cheering in a good-natured mood. As we left the performance area at the end of the ceremony, it was a reality check to see two lines of barbed-wire fencing stretching into the distance between the two countries.

Getting back to the car was a slow process because of the crowds, but we were also hindered by many Indians wanting to have their photos taken with us Europeans, especially Christian, with his light blonde hair.

The last stop was the Golden Temple, the most revered Sikh temple in India, said to be on a par with the Taj Mahal for its beauty. The temple was exquisite, dressed in its night illuminations and appearing to float like a jewel above the surrounding lake. Over 100,000 people visit the holy shrine daily to worship and partake in the free community kitchen meal.

Day two saw me struck down with a case of 'Delhi belly' (already!) and I spent most of the day in bed. The nearest chemist was closed because it was Sunday, and I felt too ill to look for another. "No problem", said the hotel manager, "I will send someone to get medication for you". A messenger boy was dispatched but shortly phoned to tell him the chemist didn't have the pills I wanted. "They must have them", I said, "They're for diarrhoea". With not a shred of embarrassment the very young manager looked me in the eye and enquired, "Loose motions?" "Yes", I said, having lost all sense of dignity by now. The pills arrived and I slept most of the day.

That evening I received an email from my daughter with the sad news that Anne Mustoe, my heroine and inspiration, had died after a short illness, whilst cycling in Aleppo in Syria. I was fortunate enough to meet her earlier in the year, and she told me she was planning to cycle from London to Singapore. She set off some weeks before I did and I often wondered where she was and how she was coping at the age of seventy-six. I'm so thankful I told her how she had inspired me – a great woman whose legacy will live on.

I was feeling a little better the next morning, and took a cycle rickshaw to the Hall Bazaar in the city centre. There, I found a road atlas of India and walked the mile or so back to my hotel, checking out bicycle repair shops on the way. There was no shortage of them, so I was reassured that help was close by if I had any problems getting Sofi back in working order. The streets were full of stalls selling food and drink, and I couldn't resist buying two freshly crushed fruit drinks along the way. They were served in dubiously-rinsed-out glasses and contained added sugar syrup and salt. In spite of my doubts about the hygiene aspect, I reasoned they would give me a good energy boost. At a chemist shop, I bought more Imodium tablets and was even able to buy antibiotics over the counter for a few rupees. A nearby outdoor stall was selling well-worn second-hand dentures. I didn't want to ask where they'd come from.

Tuesday was the day to tackle rebuilding the bike. One option was to simply take it to the bike shop across the road, but I decided to get as much done as I could and then call in the professionals if needs be. It all went well, apart from adjusting the brakes. The back tyre was also flat, so I crossed the road to get the puncture fixed and the brakes adjusted. The work was done the same day and cost me 150 rupees – just over two English pounds.

I left Amritsar early on a foggy morning, glad to escape the pall of pollution that hangs over the city. Traffic wasn't too heavy, and with the aid of directions from a helpful Sikh, resplendent in his pale green turban and elaborately-combed moustache, I soon found myself on the Grand Trunk Road. Cycling turned out to be a continual obstacle course. I had thought Iranian drivers were manic, but they had nothing on Indian drivers. The roads are a cacophony of vehicle horns, and trucks even have lettering on the rear, telling drivers behind to "Blow Horn". Buses especially seem to want to blare out to let everyone know they are there.

Stopping for a break wasn't easy, partly because of the litter and dust and partly because of the attention I was receiving. When I pulled into the side of the road, a car stopped to ask if I needed help and then two young boys came to watch me eating crisps and drinking water. They didn't speak to me, but just stood and watched in fascination. At no time did I feel threatened; it was more of a nuisance than anything else and I was becoming reluctant to stop. Most of the next fifty miles was done in one stretch, and as the day progressed, traffic increased – could I keep it up? The Grand Trunk Road is one of the busiest roads in India, so perhaps it was only to be expected. I was sure I'd work out a strategy before too long.

India was already filling me with joy and despair. The people are so friendly it is humbling, but the poverty is enough to induce anger and frustration. Some are educated and drive expensive cars, whereas others are lucky to own a bicycle. The roadsides are covered in litter, some of it fresh, some burnt to ashes and some still smouldering. Children pick among it to retrieve anything that can be recycled. I passed huts and shacks whose inhabitants had few or no possessions, and women and children who were busy forming cakes of manure to dry out for fuel. Men carried impossible loads on bicycles, and vehicles bulged at the seams with the number of passengers inside them and at the same time had as many more again clinging to the outside.

I left Jalandhar and headed for Ludhiana through another foggy morning. On the highway, I saw the body of a man on the hard shoulder lying prostrate, bare feet sticking out of a blanket. I was afraid he was dead and stopped, wondering what to do. After a while, another cyclist came along and when I gestured in the direction of the body, he shook his head at me in a way that said, "Don't get involved". Part of me wanted to lift the blanket off the man's face to check if he was alive, but I feared that if he was asleep it might shock him into striking out at me. What could I do if he was in fact dead? I convinced myself that I was not in a position to help and in any case, he was probably only sleeping. However, I later reformed my opinion and I'm sure now that he was dead, probably a casualty of the crazy traffic.

In Ludhiana, I got tangled up in flyovers and roundabouts in spite of some very helpful directions, so I continued on the Chandigarh road looking out for a hotel. People were pleased to talk to me and unabashed to brightly say "Hello" as I passed, so unlike the furtive "Hello" in Iran. They appeared to be proud of the fact that they could interact in a small way with a foreigner.

Eventually, after seeing a couple of very shabby hotels, I found one that suited and checked in. I'd cycled sixty-three miles and was filthy from the dusty road; my hands and nails were black. The shirt I'd been wearing since Calais was now so rotten with sun and sweat it had to go. A shower revived me and I went down for dinner. I had a meal of butter chicken and a bottle of beer, but later regretted the beer when I woke with stomach cramps in the night.

On the Chandigarh road the next morning, I stopped at a roadside stall to buy juice from an enthusiastic lad waving handfuls of oranges at me. He juiced the fruit and added a hefty spoonful of pink salt which destroyed any orange flavour, but it was refreshing all the same. A couple of miles further on, I saw something that defied belief. Coming towards me was a motorbike with a 'driver', if you could call him that, standing – yes, standing upright on the pillion with his hands in his pockets, speeding towards me on the opposite side of the road, among the oncoming traffic. As cool as a cucumber he flew past and disappeared into the distance behind me. I picked my jaw up of the ground and wondered if that pink stuff in my orange juice had really been salt. When I arrived in Chandigarh, I mentioned this in the hotel just to check I wasn't dreaming, and no, I wasn't. It was well known that some bikers did this dangerous stunt. Later the same day, I saw another example of what you could call unorthodox driving behaviour. Two motorbikes were almost side by side but with one a couple of feet in front of the other. The back rider had his leg locked and his foot on the back of the first bike, pushing it along.

Compared to what I'd seen of India up to now, Chandigarh felt like another world. The city was the first of Le Corbusier's urban designs to be executed and it has a surreal feel to it, especially in the context of a country like India. Built on a grid system, and with straight roads and neatly manicured grassy roundabouts, it has none of the chaos of the other towns. Streets are not named and areas are defined by sector, each with a green lawn area oriented longitudinally and stretching centrally along the sector. Based on a national government study, the city was reported to be the cleanest in India in 2010 and is said to be the 'Wealthiest Town' of India, but in spite of this obvious affluence, men still slept on the boarded sidewalks with only a blanket as bedding.

My hotel was reasonably priced and pictures of the holy man Sai Baba adorned the walls. I wandered out in the evening and visited two or three clothes shops. My trousers were becoming loose and it was time to find some that fit. In the ladies stores there was nothing practical to wear, and, in spite of my reduced waistline, all the fashionable garments were too tight. I gave up and sought out the nearest internet café.

A more cramped establishment I had never seen. The room held twelve computers, each arranged on two shallow shelves. One shelf was barely wide enough to accommodate the keyboard and the other, a flat-screen monitor. There was just enough space to sit in front of the shelves and it was as much as I could do to keep my elbows from hitting the dividing partitions. The keys on the keyboard were often unresponsive, and the atmosphere was so stifling I was glad to be kicked out at 7.30 when the place closed.

The next day, I set off on foot to see some of the architectural highlights of the city. The geometric road signs with their lines, circles and numbers were, at the same time, simple and baffling, and in the end I resorted to taking local transport. Cycle rickshaw drivers are at the bottom of the public transport scale and they were constantly asking if I wanted a ride. If I gave them my trade instead of the motorised buggies, it seemed mean to only pay them the twenty rupees they asked. I could tell how hard they worked to haul me and the cart around, because I knew how difficult it was to carry my panniers. In the end, I took a rickshaw and paid the driver double. I could have taken a motorised cab, paid the same and got there much quicker. Such is life.

In the afternoon, I had the best ten-rupees-worth of entertainment ever. This was in the Nek Chand Fantasy Rock Garden. The park covers twenty-five acres and is a maze of amphitheatres, man-made alleyways, sculptures, tunnels, bridges and waterfalls. It is a complete work of art in its use of recycled materials such as bottle tops, broken pottery and industrial porcelain, all fashioned into figurines, animals and wall decorations. I walked around admiring the panoramas and began to realise I was the centre of attention again. I would never have thought I could make so many people happy just by being a white woman in a foreign land. The garden was full of Indian tourists thrilled to speak to an English person. They waved, smiled, said hello, and wanted to take my photo. Their broad smiles were so infectious that I found myself wearing a permanent grin on my face as well.

That night, I ate at a Japanese restaurant to try and vary my diet, but slept badly and woke with stomach cramps. Was it the food or the cheap wine?

Forty miles out from Chandigarh, hotels were thin on the ground. I rode into the drive of the Red Hut complex and a Sikh wedding was in full flow with everyone immaculately dressed and a band playing bagpipes. I felt completely out of place amongst the elegant guests, but my 'Englishness' seemed to override my appearance and the uncle of the groom, in his beautiful mint green turban and dark blue blazer with brass buttons, was eager to chat to me about England.

In the restaurant that evening, my waiter spoke fluent English and was keen to talk politics. He was of the opinion that in India no one helps the poor and the rich get richer. Our conversation came round to my trip and he was very impressed, telling me that Indian women do nothing when they get older, just sit and get fat. When I asked him if women ever cycled, he said "No, cycling is for poor people". As we talked, a mouse scurried across the floor and caught my attention. It was no problem to the waiter. "Mice are very special in Indian culture", he informed me.

The next day, I was feeling queasy again and the forty-five miles to Saharanpur was hard going. After some haggling at the hotel over a room with a shower, I checked in and freshened up. I had a short rest and went out to see if I could find a supermarket, but the main street was lined with automotive shops. This had to be the dustiest town I'd seen, or perhaps Chandigarh had made the rest look worse. Pigs roamed loose, rooting among never-ending piles of litter. I returned to my room after an unproductive search.

My appetite was dwindling and I knew I was coming down with the dreaded 'bad guts' again. I spent a day in bed and on the second morning, had half an idea of leaving and trying to ride it off. Further consideration of what lay outside, the thought of manoeuvring between the hundreds of cycles, motorbikes, cars, cows and pigs made me realise that I would need all my wits about me just to get out of town. Things were bordering on serious, so I booked myself in for another night and asked the receptionist to call a doctor. Within an hour, he arrived and examined me, after which he gave me two antibiotics, two painkillers, two anti-flatulence pills and told me I had a virus and should eat plain rice for a couple of days. Feeling a lot less than convinced with the diagnosis or the treatment, I paid his £3.50 bill.

India

A Runaway Buffalo

On my first day of cycling in India, I realized there are only two rules of the road: Rule number 1 – Try not to hit anything. Rule number 2 – Try not to get hit. Unfortunately, I was about to break rule number 2.

I didn't feel brilliant when I left Saharanpur, but I wasn't ill enough to warrant another full day in bed and set off, praying that my innards would hold together until the next hotel. I could only eat one slice of toast for breakfast and packed the rest for lunch. On the way out of town, I bought a couple of bananas which I ate in the first hour.

The road was appalling for much of the way; a nerve-jangling broken surface when there was one, and not too kind on my delicate tum.

Halfway to my destination, and in amongst the general din of the traffic, I heard the sound of hooves behind me and a man shouting. My first instincts were that it was a horse-drawn cart, going by the speed of the clip-clops. In the next split-second, there was a buffalo running beside me pulling a trailer, with the driver stood on the front, whipping the animal and shouting loudly. Now – he was either shouting, 'Get out of the way – runaway buffalo!!' or, he was late for his lunch, but in the nanosecond I glimpsed his face, I'd put my money on the former. I had no time to get out of the way as the wheels of the trailer dragged at my panniers and I was thrown off the bike.

As I landed, I looked up and saw the driver looking back at me in panic. He had no chance of stopping to find out if I was alright until he had the beast under control.

I sat on the road, trying to work out what had happened and what was hurting, while a number of vehicles stopped to look at me. Strangely enough, no-one came to help, possibly because they didn't speak English and could see I was fully conscious. I was also still getting cheery 'Look-at-the-mad-English-woman' waves from some of the passing cars. After a few minutes, I stood up to pull the bike upright and get it off the road, but my head spun and I had to sit down again. I was also feeling sick and the fact that I'd had very little to eat probably didn't help. Worse than that, in an untimely fashion, the world was about to drop out of my bottom. I tried a few more times and when my head stopped spinning, I was able to stand up. By then, two or three people had stopped to ask if they could help. As far as I could see, it was either a case of calling an ambulance, or sorting myself out, and I didn't think I'd broken anything.

The onlookers left and I wheeled Sofi down a slope to find cover and did the necessary evacuation. I returned to the road, drank some soda and sucked on a boiled sweet to up my sugar levels. Inspecting the damage, I found a nasty graze on my right arm and another on my right shin – but I'd taken most of the force on my right buttock (ouch!). Sofi looked ok, although the front panniers had been dragged off the down-bars on the rack. Intact but fairly dazed, I righted myself and set off again in the direction of Muzaffernagar. I was still feeling shaken when I stopped at a hotel and kicked out my bike-stand, only to hear a resounding 'clank', as it fell off.

In the restaurant, I felt I ought to find something to eat that wouldn't make my digestive system worse, and ordered clear chicken soup and a cheese sandwich. When the soup came, it was basically a stock cube with some diced chicken thrown in – exactly what I needed – hot, wet and loaded with salt.

My encounter with the buffalo added to the daily experiences of life on the road in India, and warned me to take heed of shouting drivers. I also began to regret having no mirror on my bike.

Amongst other things, I was learning the language of the horn – I had to, to stay alive. Basically, anyone on a bicycle must get out of the way of any other vehicle. Trucks and buses are at the top of the hierarchy and blare out ear-piercing trumpeting when they are overtaking. My mantra of 'they're not allowed to kill me' didn't seem to hold in India, and I came to the conclusion that if a horn was sounded and a cyclist was hit, the motorised vehicle would be in the right.

In busy towns it was safer, because in the centre there are more bicycles than anything else on wheels. Large vehicles are trapped and can't do much, other than make a loud noise at the slow-moving traffic. In towns, I learned to thread and weave like a local – or maybe the locals were just skilful at avoiding me.

Dual carriageways are relatively safe because they usually have a wide shoulder. It's the many miles of single carriageway that pose the greatest threat to cyclists, because you have to keep manoeuvring on and off the edge of the road. A bicycle that doesn't get out of the way risks life and limb; if they're coming through, they're coming through. This wouldn't be such a problem if it wasn't for the fact that there can sometimes be a foot-high drop from the tarmac to the dirt track running alongside.

Cars, taxi-buses and motorbikes were less aggressive. Many wanted to slow down and stare at me, or indeed chat, making them usually less of a danger. Even so, they still blew their horns from behind and I had to work out what was coming.

Other cyclists could be quite amusing. None of the bikes have gears so they squeak and grind and rattle, and in general I could travel faster than they did. Sometimes a cyclist would overtake in order to give me a good looking at, but then I'd overtake him. Occasionally, I'd sense there was someone sitting on my tail and, sure enough, a bike was behind, keeping up with me. Young boys were the funniest as they seemed to think that they should be able to ride faster than me. They'd pedal hard to pass and when they thought they'd lost me they'd slow down. Up I'd pop again, turning my wheels slowly and steadily and watching my speedometer hardly changing at all. This could be repeated many times by the same boy.

Motorcyclists had a habit of talking to me at rather awkward times. When the road surface had disintegrated and I was busy trying to avoid potholes, it was most disconcerting. Questions limited to – 'Which country?' 'Where are you going?' 'Do you like India?' 'What is your name?' took quite an effort to answer politely.

I was asked my age more times than I can remember. It didn't bother me and I said I was sixty because it was easier to grasp than fifty-nine. If I stopped for a break in the day, I could guarantee that before long, a crowd would gather and watch me as I ate – a bit off-putting at first, but eventually I got used to it. I once counted twelve people in an audience.

Street food was available but there was none that looked safe to eat in my condition. I packed toast from breakfast and bought fizzy drinks, biscuits, sweets, crisps and bananas. This would keep me going until the next hotel. A balanced diet would be a long way off.

One day, I had what I call my 'Whistle Down the Wind' moment, reminding me of a scene in the fifties film of that name, with the actor Alan Bates and Hayley Mills. I was cycling along the unfinished side of a dual carriageway upgrade with other cyclists, motorbikes and the odd car, and stopped for a break. I took out bananas and biscuits and a bottle of Mountain Dew ('tain' always pronounced as in train by the Indians) and sat down. Looking across to the central reservation, I saw four young boys sit down to watch me doing whatever an English cyclist does – nothing is too mundane. They sat and I sat and then two small girls approached on my side of the road. It only took me saying "Hello" to them and the boys ran across to join the girls and gape at me at closer quarters. They tried to talk to me in Hindi, but I made it clear that I only spoke English. Undeterred, they were joined by more small children and mutely stared as I ate. As I looked at the silent wide-eyed group, I wouldn't have been surprised to hear one say, "Are you Jesus?"

Another day, I was pedalling along and saw a rare sight – a supermarket. At first I thought I must be mistaken, but no, it had all the obvious clues, glass doors, pictures of food in the window, and so on. It was only the second one I'd seen in India and wasn't in the middle of a town this time. I wheeled my bike up to lean it on a wall (it was SO unhandy not having a stand), and the forecourt attendant advised me to lock it, so I did. I walked through the shop entrance and the attendant and three other staff members followed me, not only into the supermarket but also along the aisles, as I picked out biscuits and nuts and soda. Up the next aisle they stuck like glue, but then I surprised them and made a dash for the kitchen shelves to look for a sponge (good for getting oil off your legs). I took my goods to the till and there they were again, watching me intently. The boy at the checkout entered the contents of my basket on the till and then asked for my name, which he also entered. I handed over the princely sum of 132 rupees (£1.50) and was given three feet of paper receipts which I tried to leave at the till, but no, I was told I would need them on the way out. As I reached the exit, a security man took the receipt from me to prove that I'd paid. I left the shop in a daze.

Things were not going too well as I carried on east with a deteriorating state of health. Hotels were scarce and standards were low. Dust and pollution from the traffic hung in the air permanently and the locals passed by with scarves wrapped across their faces. By the end of every day, my clothes were filthy and I needed to shower and wash my hair. Sofi was covered in dust, as were my panniers, and when I could, I wheeled her into my hotel bathroom to hose everything down, including myself.

Birdlife in India constantly fascinated me. Stopping to capture a shot of a kingfisher or an egret made a welcome distraction from the continuing grumbling in my bowels. Telegraph poles lined the side of the road and smaller birds would remain perched on the wires long enough for me to take a handful of photographs. Green bee-eaters, black drongos, mynah birds and a rare jungle owlet were added to my collection. My favourite was the Indian roller. Its colour at rest was a deceptively unimpressive brown, but when it took to the air, its wings flashed bold stripes of deep blue and bright turquoise – a spectacular display.

On the way to Moradabad, I passed a luxury hotel and couldn't resist a closer look. It was too early in the day to stop but something made me ride through the gates and up the long driveway, where a valet waited to greet guests. He politely directed me to park my bike out of sight. I walked up the steps in my dusty clothes, into a granite and mirrored reception hall of palatial dimensions. I was seriously tempted. The price for a room was seventy-five pounds – horrendously expensive by Indian standards, but by western ones it wouldn't have broken the bank. I stood and considered for some time, and came to the conclusion that staying there would only make things much harder for the following night. I regretfully declined the room and pressed on.

A few days later it rained throughout the day and I was cycling in full waterproofs. The dust on the tarmac turned to mud, spraying up from the traffic and splattering me. The roadsides became quagmires from the feet of pedestrians. It was late afternoon when I called at the first hotel on the outskirts of Shajahanpur and saw the manager emerge from a comfortable lounge. He gave me a price which I thought was too high so I moved on to see what the centre of town had to offer. Back on the road, a bundle of sugar cane fell from a passing truck and I stopped to pick up a stick, stepping in a mound of thick mud as I reached for it. By now I didn't care. The rest of the bundle was soon picked up by the locals. I'd seen people chewing on the cane many times but hadn't tried it myself.

The roadsides in Shajahanpur were filled with dozens of small wooden stalls, and in the centre, two run-down hotels didn't tempt me. I turned back to head for the first on the outskirts and the heavens opened. Pedalling through the torrential downpour, the scene around me looked as if I'd stepped into the middle ages; everything was brown – brown roads, buildings, people, shacks, animals – everything was covered in mud. By the time I got back to the first hotel, I was soaked and filthy. I politely removed my saturated trainers and waterproof trousers and very soon lived to regret it. My first impression of the place had been badly misplaced. It was a filthy hole where the proprietor managed to extract 1500R from me. My room was so disgusting I didn't want to buy his food and instead ate two bananas and a guava and had a suck on the sugar cane for supper. The bedding was dirty and smelled so sweaty that I slept in my sleeping bag on top of my roll mat. I rose at 6am the next morning and packed my bags. In the lobby, I disturbed the night watchman who was sleeping on the floor, and to add insult to injury, he ran after me demanding to know whether I had paid or not. I pedalled off feeling robbed. The road was quiet and misty as I left, and a beautiful view of the sun rising over Uttar Pradesh was my only consolation.

In Sitapur, I stopped to ask a woman if she could direct me to a hotel. Bina was outside her clothing repair shop and Sanjeev, her husband, immediately jumped on a bicycle to show me the way. With his wife sitting side-saddle on the pannier rack, I was instructed to follow him. We rode for two kilometres through street after street to a hotel, where I booked in. Sanjeev wanted to return later to show me an internet café but I declined his offer, saying it was too much to ask. "It is no trouble," he said "I am a servant of God and it is my duty to help others and spread the Gospel". He left me his name and number and asked me to pray for him and his wife.

I spent two days in Lucknow, not specifically to see the town but because I needed some rest in a decent hotel. I remembered Lucknow from school history lessons and paid a visit to the British Residency, where the famous Siege of Lucknow took place during the Indian Rebellion of 1857. Its damaged remains are a testimony to the bombardment it received during a sustained assault, but now it is a peaceful place with lovely gardens frequented by courting couples.

When I set off for Kanpur the next morning, the traffic was the worst I'd seen, a total gridlock of every type of vehicle and a sea of bicycles with me in the middle. I exited the town on a fairly good road with a narrow hard shoulder and only had to dive off a few times as buses blared past me at full pelt. I crossed the Ganges once again, and as I reached the far side, a loud bang made me wonder if a bomb had gone off. At the end of the bridge, a crowd had gathered, and peering through it, I saw what had caused the noise – a truck had toppled over the side of the bridge onto the road below. I was to see many overturned trucks and buses before I left the country.

My mood was deteriorating and I wondered if I'd ever make it to Kolkata. My insides were constantly erupting and the noise and filth were getting to me. Watching people, dogs, cows and pigs rummage through the piles of rubbish, I was beginning to question my purpose there. When I thought about the large portion of India's population with nowhere to sleep and very little food, what I was doing seemed nothing short of frivolous.

In a gloomy mood, I booked into a 3-star hotel in Kanpur. There I got a whopping 15% discount, and joy of joys – a sprung mattress, (I hadn't slept on one since Turkey. Once again, my evening meal wasn't quite what I expected. I asked for macaroni cheese, hoping for something bland, but it turned out to be full of spice and not much cheese.

On the internet that evening, I reserved two nights in a tourist hotel in Varanasi for the 24th and 25th December. There were no rooms free after that, but I would try and stay another couple of days if I could find a room. I was ready for a long break.

I slept well in my comfy bed and in the morning my spirits lifted. The manager told me he'd seen me cycling the day before and was so impressed that breakfast was complimentary. He then went on to tell me about his unsuccessful efforts to move to England. Maybe he thought I could help, but he didn't ask. He did tell me that I wouldn't find a nice hotel in Fahtepur, my next stop.

I rejoined the Grand Trunk Road with the usual carry-on of young cyclists sitting on my tail as I rode along. I decided to play one at his own game and hung back behind him. From my average of 11mph, which he'd clung to for a couple of miles, I slipped back to 6mph. The young boy had to overtake and glanced back at me every thirty seconds, obviously to see what I was playing at. I got bored with this game after a while and sped off ahead leaving him behind.

As the Kanpur manager predicted, the hotel in Fahtepur was grim – another night on the bed in my sleeping bag. The owner was pleasant enough and told me it was the best I would get before Allahabad. This time, at 500 rupees, it sufficed. There was nowhere to eat however, and I dined on fruit and biscuits before turning in. At 7.30 the next morning, I had to wake the staff sleeping on the office floor, to unlock the door and let me out.

Back on the Grand Trunk Road around 11am, I was trying to get a good shot of a pied kingfisher perched on the overhead cables, when a motorcycle driven by an educated young man stopped to talk politics. I nodded and frowned and shook my head in all the right places, wishing I could get back to my photography, and eventually, a crowd of around twenty people gathered, some on cycles, others on foot and some pulling trailers. The educated man told me I needed to eat lots of guavas because they were full of essential amino acids. With that, he promptly sent one of the onlookers off to collect some from a tree across the nearby field. It struck me at the time, just how biddable that person was. An unspoken hierarchy existed between the educated and the uneducated, which gave the former the right to give orders and be obeyed. Was this the caste system in practice? I left with seven guava fruits in my front pannier. I don't even like them that much.

I hadn't got much further when yet another motorbiker approached me, saying "Hello, my name's Dav and I'm a journalist". It crossed my mind that he may be the press, but then, it could just have been his way of greeting foreigners. He asked me what I was doing and when I told him, he asked if I would give him a bite. Well, I'd been surviving for the last two days on bananas, biscuits, sweets and Fanta, and had very little food to offer, but no, it turned out he wanted to film me for his TV channel ETV. Again, a large crowd gathered and I was hemmed in on all sides as he took out his microphone. 'At this rate…,' I wondered, '…will I ever get to Kolkata?'

If I thought my progress was slow, it was nothing to that of the men who crawl to the holy city of Varanasi. Hindu scriptures suggest that the virtue of a visit to this city is increased if the pilgrim makes the journey arduous. On two occasions, I saw a man measuring his length, face down on the road, with a stone in his outstretched hand. When he rose, he left the stone on the road, placed his feet next to it, picked it up and lay on the road again with the stone ready to reposition with his outstretched hand. The whole journey from his home to Varanasi was taken in this manner. A fair bit slower than cycling.

I reached Allahabad after seventy-five miles, at around 4pm. It was an interesting city but I didn't have time for sightseeing because it was the 22nd of December and I had to reach Varanasi by Christmas Eve. One of the benefits of staying in a more expensive hotel was that I stood a better chance of eating in a nice restaurant, so I took a room in the very posh Khana Shyam and ordered a meal. It had been some time since I last ate well and I was ready for some good food. My daytime diet of fruit, sweets and soda was becoming a worry and I had to get something nourishing inside. I dined once again on cheese pasta, but this time it wasn't so spicy. It was followed by a fresh fruit salad of papaya, banana, apple and guava. Breakfast the next day was scrambled eggs, toast, fresh fruit, tomatoes and cucumbers, washed down with lemon tea. This was the best food I'd had for some time.

Well behind schedule because of a puncture, I found my way out of Allahabad and back onto National Highway 2, as the Great Trunk Road is also known. When a motorcyclist stopped to talk to me on the way, I was grateful to be told that there was a 'hotel' called Rajput Dhaba on my route at Gopiganj. Dhabas are basically what we would know as truck stops for heavy-goods vehicle drivers, and any I'd seen didn't look so tempting. "A nice hotel?" I asked, fearing the worst, – "Oh yes", he said.

I cycled on, hoping to see something along my route which would signify the existence of accommodation. Nothing stood out and every sign was written in Hindi. Eventually, I reached a busy town which looked as if it could be Gopiganj. Whilst following the Grand Trunk Road, many of the towns looked as if numerous buildings had been cleared for its construction. Four feet high concrete barriers separated the inhabitants from the expanse of six lanes of traffic and generous shoulders. Many of the buildings next to the barriers had broken walls almost as if they'd been 'trimmed' to fit the remaining available space, but still the residents filled them with stalls or mats to sell their wares. In some towns, the vendors even spilled over the wall and laid out their goods on the hard shoulder. Others erected high poles against the barrier to hang merchandise on.

The shoulder was clear on my side and I leaned over to ask the crowd if I was in Gopiganj. Smiling children jumped up against the wall to say "Hello" and a group of women gathered to help, although no one spoke English. The further east I travelled along this main artery, the less chance I had of meeting the educated classes who might speak my language. Amongst much concern and laughter, I established that I had missed Gopiganj and was now in Aunrai, five miles past the dhaba. There was nothing for it but to turn back.

One of the customs in India is to chew the betel nut, the juice of which gives a kick similar to caffeine. To dispose of the fibrous remains after chewing, the men have mastered the art of projectile spitting, and the sputum which emanates from their mouths is bright red. Consequently, the lips and gums of the chewers are deeply stained and it is a bit disconcerting when you are talking to a man who looks like he is wearing badly-applied lipstick. To westerners, it is a disgusting habit and as I entered the dhaba restaurant, I noticed large patches of the floor were stained with the same red juice. It didn't look promising.

As it turned out, things weren't as bad as I first thought, either that, or I was beginning to lower my standards even further. The proprietor and staff were polite and friendly and although the 'deluxe' room left a lot to be desired, I could tell the grey sheets and pillow-cases had been washed in a fashion. They still carried the odour of previous occupants, so I slept inside my sleeping bag once more, but even then, I couldn't get away from the smell of sweat from the bed itself. Dhabas are used by truck drivers and workmen and I only paid 200 rupees for the night. At least I had a room to myself – I could see into other rooms which had three men sharing. I was safe and warm(ish) and had a roof over my head. At that price it was fine; in any case, who should complain when so many people in India are sleeping on the streets? I had a bed, a squat toilet, a tap, and a bucket. Sofi was in the room with me and I gave her a wash down to remove some of the grime from the roads.

Supper tonight was crisps, biscuits and nuts and again, that Indian favourite, Mountain Dew. In my small, malodorous room, I spent the evening transferring photographs to my netbook before curling up for the night. I drifted into sleep, listening to traffic blaring past outside and men honking and spitting indoors. The next morning I set off for Varanasi.

India

The Holy City

Compared to the other cities I'd seen, Varanasi was complete and utter mayhem. It was full of tourists, the majority of them pilgrims and I was stopped repeatedly by men wanting to take me to a hotel. The Scindhia Ghat, where I was staying, was on the river front and I followed signs for the ghats, the name for the broad flights of steps that lead down to the Ganges. What I didn't know was that paved roads run out well before the river and turn into a maze of narrow alleys. The crowds were getting denser and denser and when I got off the bike to walk, a rickshaw crashed into me, pulling one of my back panniers off the rack. Fortunately, there wasn't any damage, but when an elderly chap offered to lead me to my guesthouse, I was happy to pay him the fifty rupees he asked for. I wouldn't have found the hotel on my own. Had I known its location, I would never have booked to stay in a ghat-side hotel. Warrens of crowded alleyways open onto the ghat steps, and to reach the hotel door, I had to unload Sofi and manhandle her and my bags up and down numerous flights. After surviving the steps and the crush of people, I paid my guide the fifty rupees and settled into my room. When I came down to reception twenty minutes later, there was the old chap who guided me, trying to extract further commission from the manager, saying he hadn't been paid for bringing him a customer. He disappeared when he saw me.

The room was very comfortable and overlooked the Ganges. Monkeys roamed the balconies and I was instructed to keep the door of my bedroom closed to keep them out. From my balcony, I looked down on the steps and terraces where people come to bathe in the water of the sacred Ganges to wash away a lifetime of sins. Sacred to the Hindus, Buddhist and Jains it may be, but it is also among the five most polluted rivers in the world. I wasn't tempted to take a dip.

Many of the hotel guests were English speakers and it was a pleasant change to be able to converse easily. Food and drink in the hotel restaurant was good, but the service was straight out of Fawlty Towers. Customers had to write down their orders on a pad together with the room number. When one customer asked how long their meal would be, the chef barked, "I haven't much time!" My meal arrived in an haphazard order. I was firstly served a salad, then a banana and chocolate pancake, followed by a cheese and tomato toastie. When I complained to the waitress about the order of delivery, I was told abruptly, "Well I'm not the cook!" But in India there's no point in getting worked up about such things. The world turns completely differently in this country; it's best to sit back and enjoy the experience for what it is.

On Christmas Eve, a few of us took a boat trip along the river. Soon after we embarked, a smaller vessel drew aside and we were sold candles to float on the surface of the water while asking Mother Ganges to grant our wishes. The next day, Christmas Day, I walked along to the Burning Ghat to watch bodies being cremated on funeral pyres. I had long thought that such a ceremony would be the best way to depart this earth and was intrigued to find out if I still felt the same on witnessing the reality. Seeing families gathered to watch fires blaze, as the remains of their loved ones turned to smoke and ash, confirmed my feelings.

On Boxing Day, I woke at 5am to join fellow guests Jean and Wim on an early morning boat trip. It was pitch-black when we left at 5.30 and Mr Moon, our boatman, rowed us down the river to watch the dawn breaking. By 6am, dramatic colours flooded the scene, changing every minute. The sun rose as a bright white orb, encircled by a blushing red aura, and a brilliant ladder of reflections adorned the ripples on the Ganges below. Fishing boats were silhouetted against the pale light, and blues, pinks and oranges began to bathe the water where moored boats bobbed. The bankside ghats in reds, ochres and browns were at their loveliest as the Sun rose higher in the sky. Through sleepy eyes, the experience was like a dream. I was so glad I hadn't missed it.

I managed to eat a few meals but was still unable to shake off the bugs that had taken up residence in my stomach. I spent four nights in Varanasi and rested most of the time. In the daytime, I would walk the narrow alleys lined with shops and marvel at how on earth the infrastructure held together. The lanes are no more than ten feet wide and crammed with people, cows, bicycles and even the odd motorbike squeezing through.

The bodies of the dead also make their way to the Burning Ghat along these corridors, carried on shoulder-high stretchers by the lowest castes or Dalits. It's not quite as gruesome as it sounds, as the deceased are covered in brightly coloured shrouds. Wood for the pyres is brought up the river, and behind the Burning Ghat, vendors sell the logs individually by weight to only the wealthiest of relatives of the dead. The Dalits live in a segregated part of the village and are not allowed to use the wells, temples and facilities that are used by the upper castes. They clean up the ashes after a funeral and hunt for any leftover gold, such as teeth, which may have survived the fire.

During the evenings, I was planning the next stretch of the journey, which was to Kolkata, a city with one of the highest population densities in India. The guestbook of my online journal was a great comfort, with people from all over the world sending me seasonal good wishes and empathising with my troubled digestion. It was wonderful to know that so many people were batting for me.

I left the Scindhia Ghat on 28th December by rowing boat and was taken half a mile upstream towards a bridge north-east of the city. This was the easiest way to get back on the Grand Trunk Road. The boatman stopped under the bridge, where whole families, possibly Dalits, were living in shacks built from any waste material they could find, be it wood, tin or cardboard. My guide carried my bike and we plodded through the mud and litter between the slums, up to the road above. Another half a mile and I was back on the Grand Trunk Road.

India

To Kalkota

My next stop was supposed to be Chandauli, but I reached it far too early in the day and opted to press on. Around 3pm, I saw a Bharat Petroleum service station which looked as if it might have accommodation, and crossed the dual carriageway to investigate.

The owner, a retired 'full' colonel, was having lunch and invited me to sit and talk over a cup of tea. He cut a dashing figure with his thick black hair, matching moustache and perfect English. "I will help you," he said. "We have eight-bed dormitories you can use". "Shared?" I asked, apprehensively. "No, no, you can have one to yourself." "How much?" I asked. "Oh, not much," he said, "India is very cheap – anyway, you can stay for free." An offer like that, I couldn't refuse. I listened as he talked about Pakistan, telling me, "They are all fundamentalists", and went on to say that India was different, a very free country. Neither of us mentioned the poverty or the squalor. He finished his tea, gave me a key and said goodbye, driving away in a shiny new 4x4 packed with his overweight family.

In Varanasi, I had met a couple from New Zealand, Setareh and Arjen, who had been trekking in Nepal. From Arjen, I learned that running a ceiling fan would stop the mozzies biting, as they can't fly if there is any air disturbance. Previously, I'd spent many nights wearing my anti-mosquito head-net, but the blighters still managed to pierce my skin where it touched. Here in Chandauli, I spent the night in an empty eight-bed dorm, with one of the four ceiling fans turning quietly above me on low speed. Settling down for the night was another matter, as there were no blinds or curtains in the room. Unsurprisingly, I was an object of curiosity to drivers who tried to sneak a furtive glance through the windows as they passed. With a bit of wriggling, I found I could manage a small amount of privacy if I lay horizontal behind the low partitions between the beds. I eventually, slept like a log.

Breakfast at the restaurant was a challenge. Flies were everywhere, covering a grey dishcloth hanging from a tap in the sink and swarming over the gooey necks of the sauce bottles on the tables. In spite of the buzz around, me I still needed to eat and reluctantly ordered toast and chai.

The day ahead turned out to be long, because every time I asked for directions I still managed to overshoot my destination. At a lunchtime break on the road, I was once again surrounded by onlookers. For some unknown reason, a man wrapped in a scarf put his hand out to me and said, "Thank you". He then said something about his mother and lifted the end of his scarf to gently wipe my face. My eyes had been streaming all morning from the cold wind and when I reached for a tissue, he took it from me and dabbed my cheek. I found it quite touching.

Amongst the ever present sights of poverty in India something else caused me considerable distress, and this was the state of the dogs. Dogs have the status of vermin. Every one I saw was hungry to the point of starvation, and they all suffered from varying degrees of mange. In Varanasi, I saw one animal with protruding ribs lying on the steps of a ghat, pitifully gasping its last. Cows, on the other hand, have 'sacred' status and wander among the crowds, being fed buckets of food by the locals. Later, I witnessed a very upsetting incident. As I cycled along a dual carriageway I saw a large dog lying in the fast lane ahead of me. It was sat up and alert but must have been injured, and I dreaded what I knew would happen. I didn't have long to wait before a truck hurtled towards the animal and hit it. The poor thing screamed in agony and was still screaming as I rode into the distance. There was nothing I could usefully achieve by stopping, but my ears rang with the sound of its cries.

After sixty-four miles, I finally found the road I wanted, and bumped and bounced my way over the potholes into Sasaram. It was some distance from the Grand Trunk, but it was the nearest town with the likelihood of accommodation for some miles. As I wound my way through the unpaved streets, I passed a young girl, of maybe six years old, and the astonishment on her face as she looked up was a picture. Her shock couldn't have been any greater if I'd been a Martian from outer space; and I suppose that to her I looked like one in my helmet.

A young man with betel-red lips told me to stay on the "main road" through the town. I may have been on the main road but the surface was in such bad condition, that I soon had to dismount and push until I found a reasonable hotel, the cheapest one yet at 175 rupees (£2.50). I dined at the Prince restaurant and ate chicken masala and a butter naan. It was fortunate that I'd bought a small bottle of 'Thums Up' cola on the way, as the restaurant only had tap water. This time, the ceiling fan rattled loud enough to stop me sleeping and the manager lit a mosquito repellent coil in my room which seemed to do the trick, but goodness knows what it did to my lungs.

If I thought the road into town was bad, it was even worse on the way out – full of holes and with a constant stream of tractors loaded with stone, threatening to wipe me out if I got in the way. Clouds of dust blew in my eyes and covered my clothes. My spirits were reaching an all-time low and I wondered again if I'd ever make it to Kolkata. Leaving Sasaram and returning to the relative sanity of the GTR was a welcome improvement.

The next hotel at Aurangabad was acceptable. There was no hot water and I sorely needed to shower and wash my hair, but there was no point in worrying about it. A quick cold wash sufficed, I tied my hair up in a comb and that was it. There was no change on the abdominal front and I went out to look for Imodium, but could only find more antibiotics which I bought to save for an emergency. Funnily enough, my insides seem to hang together during the day, in spite of my very strange daytime diet. Now I was on bananas, oranges, raw carrots, peanut brittle and lots of soda. Sometimes, I could find Cadbury's chocolate éclairs of all things. It was so good to put something in my mouth that had a familiar taste and I bought bagfuls when I could find them. They were sold individually at one rupee each, clearly beyond the pocket of most Indians, but to me not a lot. I bought in bulk and the stallholder would painstakingly count out thirty of them, one at a time. Only sugar was keeping me going and I vowed to make up for my poor diet at the first opportunity. I slept well until 6.50am and then went downstairs to look for breakfast, but there was none on offer. Silly me for expecting it just because it was on the menu.

The next day was New Year's Eve and by noon I'd reached Sherghati, the only town of any size for forty miles. I pondered what to do and decided to keep going. To stop cycling at noon seemed such a waste, and what would I do all day? There were no cafés or bars and not much likelihood of any internet access, so I carried on.

Twelve miles further and I spotted another Bharat Petroleum service station and thought I'd try my luck again. A dozen or so men were working there and they were all eager to help. There was some confusion when I said "Hotel?" because they thought I was looking for a restaurant. There was very little English spoken, but when it was understood that I needed somewhere to sleep, one of them brightly asked, "Night halt?" I nodded in agreement and was immediately offered a shelter to spend the night in for free. It was nothing more than a garage with an up-and-over door, tools and clothes hanging on the walls and a couple of shelves along the floor supported with bricks. The fact there was a guard asleep in it at the time was no problem and he was soon ejected unceremoniously. Luxury it wasn't, but I was touched by the unconditional offer and I needed somewhere to stay, so I thankfully accepted. Javed, the manager, and his staff carried in a fold-up bed for me – basically a hinged ply-wood board on legs. Still, I had my camping gear and it was better than being on the ground.

It was only 2pm but after my early start I was ready for a nap, so I pulled out my sleeping mat and bag and put my head down. I dozed intermittently, interrupted at intervals by workers reaching for coats beside me and one man rummaging under the shelves for a pan of curry which he ladled into a bowl. At 3pm I was fully awake and some of the workers were chatting with me in broken English. I remembered my bag of sweets and worked out that there were enough left to go round. Their faces lit up at what was evidently a treat for them. However, my calculation was based on the western custom of only taking one sweet when offered the bag and I wasn't expecting them to dive in and take a few, which is what they did. The last worker ran up to take advantage of the bounty and I had to hang on to the last one for him before the bag was emptied.

It was fairly obvious that I was in the way in the garage and I wasn't surprised when Javed upgraded me to his office. I was moved, bed, bike and bags, across the yard, and as I settled down that evening, a hot supper of veg curry, omelette, raita and naans was brought to me by two of Javed's men, Yogendar and Pandi. In spite of my protests, they wouldn't accept any payment for the meal – such hospitality to a perfect stranger and all I could offer was a bag of sweets. I looked at the meal and knew the curry wasn't a good idea but leaving it would have been an insult and as I started to eat I realised just how hungry I was.

That should have been a perfect end to my New Year's Eve but my worries about the curry were well-founded and I spent the night rushing backwards and forwards in the dark to the loo on the far side of the compound. I didn't get much rest, nor did I bargain for being woken at 6.30am by Javed who needed his office back. I said my goodbyes and thanks and by 7.15am on New Year's Day I was on the road.

For some reason, my legs kept going without too much of a struggle and eighty-four miles later, with daylight fading, I arrived at a hotel in Parasnath. The entrance had no frontage at ground level, only stairs immediately behind the door, leading to the reception and rooms. Hotels like this are always difficult for a cyclist, because it means leaving your bike unguarded, while you race upstairs to enquire. I normally try to avoid them, but here in India I had very few options. As usual, a crowd gathered to watch me as I eyed up the situation. Here was the dilemma – I could either leave my bike with the audience, hoping it was perfectly safe, or ask someone in the crowd to go up the stairs and bring down a member of staff. I chose the latter and the manager came down to carry my bike up the stairs and book me in. Below the hotel, a brightly-lit restaurant with a coal-fired stove was busily serving food. Flames were leaping from the stove and the interior of the restaurant was blackened with soot. It opened straight on to the street with no windows or doors, presumably to stop the smoke from choking the customers. Workmen eating as the stove blazed away, stared out at me with curiosity, so I walked up the street looking for some food to take back to my room. The sun had set by now and it was becoming chilly. In the light of the open shops, groups of men huddled around small fires along the earth sidewalks, warming their hands, their dark eyes shining in the reflection of the flames. The shops were really no more than kiosks and the choice of food was limited, but I was able to buy a small loaf of white bread and a small pack of butter. I'd been trying to avoid packaged bread because it was quite nasty stuff – very white and sweet. I couldn't find jam anywhere and, perhaps because my knuckles were starting to scrape the ground, I was getting a little fed up with bananas. Still, that was all I had, so I made a banana and crisp sandwich for my supper. The crisps, of course, were masala flavour.

My room reeked of soot, but in spite of the squalor, I found it difficult to rise the next day. I was snug inside my down sleeping bag and stayed there until 8am. The previous day's miles were obviously taking their toll. It was after nine by the time I got away and the cold was making my eyes stream again, even though the wind was at my back. My hands and nails were filthy and I hadn't washed my hair for two weeks.

I was now leaving the Punjab, Uttar Pradesh and Bihar behind and heading for Jharkhand. The scenery had become more undulating and I could see hills on either side through the fog. At the same time, the population density along the Grand Trunk Road had decreased, which made it easier to stop without gathering an audience. In general, people were still friendly, shouting hello and stopping me to talk. Conversation, however, had become much more limited, now with only the usual phrases of 'Where are you coming from?' and 'What is your name?', but people were still polite, cheerful and eager to help. I was riding through a coal-producing area now and coal dust coated everything, including the road and the faces of the labour force. Many men pushed bicycles laden with sacks of coal. They couldn't possibly have ridden the bikes and they leaned into the ground as they pulled their heavy loads. Chimneys lined the roadside, adding a sooty smell to the air.

My next encounter was full of promise but ended up causing me a problem. A car carrying two elderly gentlemen pulled up in front of me at a service station. One of the men got out of the car, announced that his name was Mati Baba and hung a garland of orange marigolds around my neck in appreciation of, well, just because I was on a bicycle. I was a little bemused when he asked if my Sigg water bottle was a motor. "Is there anything I can do for you?" he asked. "Do you need anything? – Money?" I was quite taken aback at this and as politely as I could, said "No". "You must join us for lunch", he replied. After explaining that I had to find a hotel in Dhanbad 10 miles off the Grand Trunk, Mati Baba said I didn't need to go there. They were going to the Hotel Khalsa for lunch, which was on the Grand Trunk Road, and they knew the owner and I could stay there. Visions of old colonial buildings crossed my mind and I imagined sitting in comfort on rattan furniture eating sandwiches and drinking tea. I agreed to meet them within the hour.

It would have been a good option, if not for the fact that the Hotel Khalsa wasn't a hotel any more, it was a restaurant. I found the two gentlemen in a room filled with families dining. Adults and children were eating in the traditional Indian way with their fingers, the tables were plastic-covered, and they and the floor were covered in food. The children were making a racket, as children do. There wasn't a rattan chair in sight. As I surveyed the scene before me, I realised I would have to back-track to Dhanbad, and leave quickly to get there before dark. My two Indian friends were indignant and insisted that I should sit down and eat while they sorted things out. "It will be fine", said Mati Baba among the noise. "I know the manager. You can stay here". They certainly weren't listening to me and I had no confidence in leaving my fate in their hands, so in spite of their protestations, I said my goodbyes and left. I'm sure they thought I was very rude, but we couldn't agree so I had no choice.

Across the highway, a dhaba was offering a filthy room with no toilet attached. I was irked by now and remember saying to myself, 'it's a shithole without a shithole', when I turned it down. I took off for Dhanbad and ten miles later, checked into the town's 3-star hotel for two nights, to rest, eat and have a jolly good wash – aaahh bliss!

The Skylark was an excellent hotel. Even though it was relatively expensive, I stayed a third night in order to get some good food inside me and hopefully settle my stomach. I ate a very good Thai curry the first two nights, and on the third, ordered a meal called a chicken sizzler. This was a hollowed out cabbage filled with breaded chicken, a whole green pepper and a tomato, both stuffed with rice, all topped with a spicy sauce of sweetcorn, green beans, carrots and tinned mushrooms. Noodles were piled over the top, and the whole lot was garnished with chips. It was a strange looking dish, but full of the sort of fresh food I had been missing in my diet. I polished off the lot.

My days were spent resting or wandering up the dusty main street, where I saw another pitiful sight. At first I noticed three dogs sleeping in the dust beside the road, but then realised there was actually a fourth. I hadn't seen it because it had no fur at all and was the same black colour as the coal dust. Curled up like a hairless foetus, its face twitched at the flies but it wasn't capable of doing any more. The next day, I saw its dead carcass had been moved away from the edge of the road.

Getting back onto the GTR from the mining town of Dhanbad took a little time but was fairly straightforward. A good day's cycling was had and I arrived in Durgapur where I was invited to do another interview for a local TV channel. Durgapur had been earlier described to me as a steel town, and for me it was the first that had any resemblance to Chandigarh. I only saw a fraction of it but the streets and buildings were immaculate. I should have spent longer there and explored, but my energy was at low ebb. I found a room and went to visit the nearby TV offices, where I was the focus of attention of the staff and interviewed by a senior journalist with orange-dyed hair.

From Durgapur, the industrial scenery rose up on either side of the highway, with mines and chimneys dotting the horizon. In some places, I passed through one breakers yard after another, all of them filled with heavy vehicles and machinery in varying states of destruction. In my weakened state I felt as if I had reached cycling hell.

At the next hotel, there was no running hot water, but that was soon addressed by a porter who brought me an electric element fastened to a wooden crossbar and a bucket – safety at its best. In the restaurant, the menu looked promising. Indeed, the vegetable soup was fresh, but if only the fish fingers hadn't been so hot and spicy! Again I was an object of curiosity for the staff, who stood and watched as I ate my meal. The next morning, they all obligingly assembled outside for a photograph, and were pleased to hear my genuine compliments about their hotel.

Leaving the town of Burdamann, I set off in the direction of Kolkata and by nightfall I was still on my bike, approaching the busy city centre anxiously looking for hotels. This was not a place to be cycling in the dark. Fortune must have been smiling on me when I happened to glance to my left and spotted a sign for the Kolkata Youth Hostel. In the dark, the heavy traffic had become intimidating and I immediately swung left, praying I could get in. There was some umm-ing and aa-ing, but to my relief I was given a room. How the manager worked out the price I don't know. It started off at 375 rupees, then went down to 300 rupees when I showed my YHA membership, then I was offered complementary dinner and breakfast and then I was given 100 rupees back..? The dinner, I was unable to accept because of my dodgy innards and I couldn't face one more plate of buttered toast and omelette for breakfast. One of the assistants found a banana which I managed to eat. The staff were a lovely lot and they came outside to wave me off the next morning with lots of good wishes.

I arrived in central Kolkata around 11am and jumped off my bike to search for Sudder Street, where I knew most of the hotels were located. After some winding around the busy streets, I was stopped by a man who looked partly Indian but spoke perfect English. This turned out to be Ray, an Anglo-Indian who had spent most of his life in London and had moved back to Kolkata to live. He was delighted to meet someone from England and helped me find a hotel. He also took me to a travel agent to book a flight and spent the next four days showing me the sights of the city. I saw parts I would never have seen on my own, including the impressive South Park Street Cemetery, with its monumentally-huge, Gothic gravestones, used by the British Empire until 1830. We visited the Victoria memorial, and some of the oldest market areas in the city, and at one acquired a cardboard box and tape for me to pack the bike.

Ray introduced me to new Indian delicacies and even ate at McDonald's with me to humour my digestive needs. One thing he pointed out about trying to eat safely was that I shouldn't have been drinking lassi. Whereas I'd been thinking the live yogurt was good for my indigestion, it hadn't occurred to me that it is diluted with tap water. It was a bit late to find out now.

One of our outings was to the local post office to send a parcel home. The staff paced leisurely behind the counter with an air of total disinterest in the customers. Eventually, I was seen by an assistant who directed me outside to get my parcel wrapped. In the sunshine sat a man who looked at my package and gave me a price. I watched as he wrapped the bundle in cotton cloth, stitched it together with needle and thread and sealed it with wax. I then had to write the address on the cotton and fill in three forms which were folded and stapled to the corners of the parcel. I was sure it wouldn't arrive in England intact, but in fact it did.

Ray and I had our last cup of tea at the Tea Junction Café, and at 12 noon we set off for the airport in a taxi, with bike, bags and box in the back. There was no space at the hotel to pack the bike in advance, so I would have to box it at the airport.

We said our goodbyes at the airport entrance and I went through to find a space to box the bike, but when one of the porters saw me starting to take Sofi apart I was turfed outside.

Dismantling it soon drew a crowd of curious men and the screech of the packing tape as I dragged it off the roll made my activity even more conspicuous. I kept my head down and carried on mummifying the box. I balanced it on a trolley in order to cover the ends, then stood it on end and walked round and round it with the tape, getting dizzy in the process.

None of the men offered to help, but a brave young Indian girl stepped up to hold the parcel as I wrapped. Most of the onlookers must have thought I was quite mad, but I was getting more and more used to that.

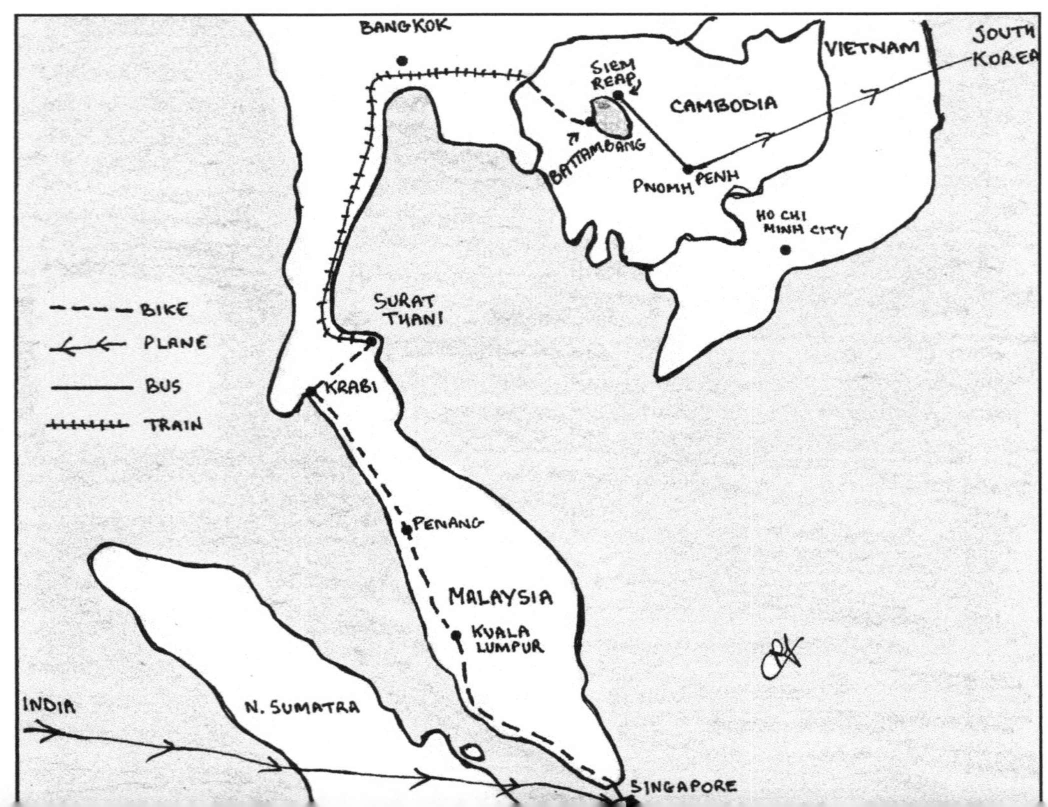
BANGKOK
SIEM REAP
CAMBODIA
VIETNAM
SOUTH KOREA
BATTAMBANG
PNOMH PENH
HO CHI MINH CITY
SURAT THANI
BIKE
PLANE
BUS
TRAIN
KRABI
PENANG
MALAYSIA
KUALA LUMPUR
INDIA
N. SUMATRA
SINGAPORE

Singapore
Time for a Haircut

It was 4am when I arrived at the sparkling Changi Airport and I hadn't slept much. But what to do at this early hour in an empty airport with all the shops closed? The obvious answer was to put the bike back together, so that's what I did. As I worked on the contents of my box, a male cleaner appeared and offered to take the cardboard away.

"Where are you going?" he asked.

"North to Thailand."

"But it's dangerous."

"I'll be fine", I replied. He walked away shaking his head.

The airport was coming to life now and I made my way to a café and ordered eggs on toast. It sounded like a typical English breakfast but the meal was disappointing because the eggs were undercooked. What I didn't know then, was that a 'half-boiled egg' is a Chinese delicacy.

My first two days in Singapore were spent trying to catch up on lost sleep and it wasn't that easy. I seemed to be buzzing with the events of the preceding days and nights and found it difficult to wind down. But sleep did come at last and I woke on Saturday, ready to hit the town on an open-topped bus. Ray and I had done a lot of walking in Kolkata and I was pleased to take the easy option this time.

Singapore has no pollution, no poverty, no litter, no noise, no traffic congestion and no crowds to speak of. The culture change was dramatic and left me gaping at the spotless shops and restaurants, and stunned by the comparative silence in the air. To see pedestrians stand and wait for traffic lights to change before crossing the road was a novelty after the total disregard for such things in India.

Ironically, I was staying in the area called Little India, simply because it was the nearest district to the airport. At least half the restaurants were Indian and I was determined to avoid the curries which I was heartily sick of. I sought out Japanese, Malaysian or western food. In such a clean environment, I was optimistic that my digestive system would quickly stabilise, but my appetite seemed to have deserted me and I could still only eat small amounts.

By now, my hair was in need of a cut and I found an Indian hairdresser. She made me respectable again but would have liked to dye what was now a white head of hair. Even though I do colour my hair, I was still enjoying an experiment to see what I looked like 'au naturel' and declined her advice.

In the famous Raffles bar I checked the price of a Singapore Sling and at first turned away in shock, but then, thinking of my friend Steve who would have said, "It's gotta be done…", I changed my mind. Throwing expense to the wind, I not only had a cocktail but ordered chicken and chips to go with it. The drink was very good, but the food was an unimpressive equivalent of a KFC meal. Still, I was there for the history and the ambience more than anything and, although the Long Bar was full of tourists, I enjoyed spoiling myself and spent time writing up my diary. There are boxes of peanuts in shells on every table and the tradition is to eat the nuts and throw the shells on the floor which makes for some interesting background noises. In my present state, I couldn't stomach any nuts. I walked back to my hotel through a flea market and picked up a pair of cropped pants for two Singapore dollars (less than one British pound). They were just what I needed for the hot climate, although it was a bit alarming to find that I needed a piece of string to hold them up.

Sofi was parked in my room and that afternoon I took her into the shower to hose her down. What a mess! – half of India was on the floor. It took me as long to clean the shower as it had the bike. Then with the front mudguard and pannier clip fixed, moving parts oiled, brakes working well and tyres pumped up, I went out for a test ride and all seemed to be in order.

Malaysia
A Steady Decline

After three nights in Singapore I headed north towards Malaysia. The route map was easy to follow and streets were clearly signed, but the cycling itself was the hardest it had been since Italy because of the heat. Temperatures in the north of India had been in the high teens, whereas South East Asia was now in the thirties. I'd forgotten just how much liquid intake was involved and had to restock before crossing the causeway across the Straits of Johor.

My small scale map of Malaysia wouldn't be much help until I hit the coastal road, but in spite of my efforts to stay close to the water's edge, the busy network of highways conspired to take me into the middle of Johor Bahru, the capital of Johor State. I asked around how to get to the coast but people didn't understand that I couldn't use the expressway. At a hectic interchange with flyovers above and fast-moving traffic on all sides, I ended up standing on an island for an eternity, at a loss for which way to turn and waiting for divine inspiration. A young Muslim girl was standing at a nearby bus stop and came to see if she could help this poor woman, but as I expected, she was unable to offer any useful advice.

I had to get off the traffic island, so I took the left lane and ended up in a residential area. By then, I'd clocked up nearly thirty miles on my bike computer and resolved to check in at the first hotel to work out a plan. I trawled the streets but no hotel materialised. A cabbie called me from a parked taxi and at first I thought he was chasing a fare. I gave my customary polite rebuttal but, thankfully, he persevered and asked me where I was going. I said I needed to find the coastal road and he told me to follow him. There was no better alternative so I rode behind him for about a mile until he stopped and gave me instructions to follow the road to my left where I would see signs to Pontian, my destination. I was so grateful and wanted to pay him but he would have none of it. Leaving him with my thanks, I soon found myself on the right road.

How beautiful the tropical countryside was. I was in a huge botanic garden full of palms, banana trees and exotic flowers. The road undulated towards the coast and the heat was sapping my energy, but still there were no signs of accommodation. I took a long diversion to one hotel but my powers of calculation must have been affected by the heat. In trying to convert 240 Malaysian ringgits, I'd arrived at £125. If I'd realised it was only £50, I was hot enough and tired enough to take it. Cycling seemed to be so hard, and it was 7pm by the time I reached Pontian and too late to shop around. I took the first hotel I saw. When I finally worked out that the price was the equivalent of £16 a night for what was a good 3-star, I was happy.

Pontian lies on the coastal road which would take me north to Thailand, and I took two days off to adjust to the new country. There was wi-fi in my room for the first time in weeks and I could do lots of much-needed domestic catching up, answering emails, updating my journal and looking after my finances. In spite of the changes in environment and food, my health wasn't picking up as quickly as I expected and, apart from a few short walks, I spent most of my days resting. To pass the time, I became inventive on the sewing front and chopped the legs off my long-since relegated best trousers and made them into a pair of shorts. On admiring them in the mirror, I couldn't help noticing how much thinner my legs looked. The miles I'd covered since entering Turkey must have taken their toll. But ye gods! – it was hot out there and I would have to keep my mileage down now, to avoid melting.

Talking of gods, making those shorts was enough to bring the gods of hubris out that night to lash the coast with an electrical storm of biblical proportions. Fortunately, by the time I was on the road the next morning, the light show was over, it had stopped raining and the air was much fresher.

My insides were still rumbling as I rode along, but there was so much to distract me in this Garden of Eden. I saw banana fruits hanging on the trees in protective bags, heaps of palm oil berries lying on the roadside waiting to be collected, trees with vicious spikes on their trunks, seed pods with beetles living inside and roadkill of all descriptions flattened on the tarmac – huge lizards and snakes and a few exotic birds.

By noon, the heat was building up and I was cooked at 2pm when I reached Batu Pahat. I was seriously dehydrated and constantly needed chilled drinks to cool me down. It seemed as if I was stopping at every opportunity to restock. A mile up the road from the last service station, two smiling girls appeared alongside me on a scooter carrying my bar-bag. How could I have left it behind without realising? How could I not notice it wasn't in front of me on the bike? Was it just the heat? I was beginning to question my sanity. I checked into a hotel and crashed for a couple of hours. In the evening, I wandered into town for a plate of chicken and rice, and plenty of green tea.

In the morning, I felt refreshed and the next thirty-three miles was a leisurely ride to Muar. Malaysia has such a relaxed atmosphere that it was easy to enjoy cycling, taking in the exotic vegetation and friendly smiles of the locals. People were happy to say hello and, even though they found me something of a curiosity, it wasn't in an impolite or invasive way. Here I saw many women riding bicycles, some in Muslim dress. One female cyclist was wearing a burka and stopped on the opposite side of the road watching me. What was she thinking? A lace grille covered her face so there was no knowing. I waved and she waved back tentatively. How I wished I'd crossed to talk to her.

The road to Melaka was fairly uneventful, apart from seeing a large fat brown lizard scuttle off into the grass and a beautiful brahminy kite, with brown upper body and white head – both disappearing too quickly to photograph. Around midday, when the sun was scorching my arms, I stopped at a wayside café for lunch and a drink of iced strawberry syrup.

I wended my way through the traffic and roadworks in Melaka and found myself a hotel – this time with resident ants. They were very tiny, only about 1mm long, but they were everywhere. I thought I'd get them to come off the walls and the bed by putting a crisp (seaweed flavour by the way) by their entry point under the door. That plan failed completely because within one minute, they'd moved the crisp two inches towards the hole, and within five minutes, it had disappeared under the floorboards. The rest just carried on running over the windows and walls. I asked the receptionist to deal with them and left to find food. Close by was a western-style shopping centre with a supermarket packed with fresh fruit and veg. When I got back to my room, the ants had gone and I chopped up a healthy salad for supper.

Melaka is a lively town with a rich history in which the British played a significant part. As part of the British Empire, Malaysia was prospering, but this came to an end during World War II when the Japanese occupied the country. The economy of Melaka is now based on tourism and a colourful night market is held on Jonker Walk, which I had to see. I had my first sugar cane drink from one of the food stalls, and a coconut rice cake called a Putu Piring. The Melaka River was lit with bright blue lights as I returned along its banks to my room. Back at the hotel, the ants had returned and were running over my keyboard and screen, very distracting when you're trying to type.

Finding my way back onto the coastal road was a struggle, and after two attempts which should have provided early accommodation failed, I ended up close to Port Dickson having cycled through most of the heat of the day. Here I was in the land of luxury resorts and after checking out a couple that were far too expensive, I was more than surprised to find myself in a studio apartment big enough to hold a large party, with breakfast and a free lunch included. I'd chanced upon a promotional offer and I decided to take full advantage and stay two nights, as I was still trying to regain my strength. It was becoming harder and harder to face the road. I'd left India with my insides churning, and since arriving in Singapore, I'd been hoping that my health would improve. Now I was experiencing bouts of feeling sick and nauseous. Much as I hated to give in, I was beginning to think I wouldn't pull myself out of the downward spiral without the help of a doctor.

Whilst in India, I'd been offered accommodation in Kuala Lumpur by one of my journal readers. This was Yoong Shee Phat or 'Peter' to give him the name he normally uses, and as the capital was on my route, I'd accepted his offer. My progress north was becoming slower and slower by the day and although I kept postponing the date I would arrive, I didn't want to let Peter down, so I felt I had to keep going.

Food was still proving to be a challenge. Unlike western menus, which differentiate between breakfast, lunch and dinner, Malaysian meals are the same throughout the day. I was longing for my morning cereal, but when I thought I'd found porridge, it turned out to be a savoury dish containing chicken. At one breakfast, I was overjoyed to see a basket of boiled eggs, only to have my expectations dashed when I cracked one and found runny white and yolk flooding my dish. I thought I'd been unlucky and tried another, but no – I was experiencing the Chinese 'half-boiled egg' again.

On the last morning at the resort, I dragged myself out of bed at 6.30, full of good intentions to set off early and beat the heat of the day. My plans were soon thwarted when I discovered I was the only person around, even though the breakfast ticket said 7am to 9am. The dining room overlooked the beach and the sun was about to appear over the distant horizon, so I wandered outside among the palm trees to watch a beautiful sunrise while I waited for the staff to wake up.

At 7.30, a flustered young man appeared and quickly cooked up baked beans, sausages and two fried eggs atop of a damp slice of bread, which was supposed to be toast. I ate the eggs and beans and one of the sausages and cycled off still feeling queasy.

A few miles along, I had my first encounter since India with an all-chatting, all-driving motorcyclist – the ones who ride alongside and open up a conversation on the move. He found it very odd that I was on my own and asked the usual questions about my journey. He then informed me that one of the reasons Westerners were able to cycle alone, was because we didn't believe in ghosts. He wasn't trying to frighten me, but leaving me with that thought and a few helpful directions, he went on his way. I found out later that there is a spooky history associated with the area I was about to ride through, and that may have been his motivation. Personally, I had too many internal gremlins giving me grief to worry about ghosts, and it wasn't long before I was in such pain that I pulled off the road, bending double over my handlebars with stomach cramps. 'This is a disaster', I was thinking – 'all the time, the clock is ticking towards meeting up with Peter, and no-one wants to arrive at a stranger's house, knowing they'll never get you out of their bathroom'. The cramps passed and I perked up a little.

Following Peter's directions, I took the N4 leading to a ferry which would take me across the river and cut short the road route by around three miles. The track on the other side wound its way into Sunga Pelek, where I spotted a Kentucky Fried Chicken and stopped to enjoy the delights of another familiar-tasting meal. I can say that without a doubt, it was better than the meal I'd had in Raffles.

A couple of miles out of town, there was a sign pointing to the left advertising two resorts but it didn't say how far they were, so I carried on in a northerly direction. How I wished I hadn't. The road turned into one that stretched ahead interminably – nothing but palm forests on either side and not a restaurant or garage for miles. I was starting to seriously wilt.

I finally arrived exhausted at a service station and asked the girl behind the counter if there was anywhere to stay.

"No hotel", she told me cheerfully, "The next one is in Morib."

"How far is it?"

"Twelve miles. It will only take you half an hour."

"Half an hour!!? In this heat!!?" Feeling very despondent, I set off. Her half hour was going to be well over an hour at my current pace. But my luck was in – within two miles I saw, not a tourist hotel, but a local resort and somewhere to lay my head.

The Bakaugruv Kampung Resort was much more interesting than any of the hotels. Accommodation was in basic woven-palm huts and its beautiful exotic grounds were a delight. Tall, spreading coconut palms leaned over ponds and durian trees grew in the gardens. A 200m jetty extended over mangrove swamps and fiddler crabs poked out of the mud. It was a fascinating place to stay.

I had arranged to meet Peter the next day, twenty miles further on at Jenjarom. I rose for breakfast but felt so weak I had to go back to bed for a lie down. When I finally set off, I only made it ten miles up the road to Morib and rang Peter. We met on the roadside and he loaded my bike and bags onto his car. "I'm afraid I'm not very well Peter", I said feebly. His reply was categorical, "You're not leaving my home until you are better." We arrived at his house and, with great understanding, the first thing he did was direct me towards the toilet.

Being unable to eat the food that was offered to me at supper was embarrassing but I couldn't face it. Instead, my angel of a host, Peter, made me porridge – not Malaysian style, but bland and sweet and a balm to my troubled digestive system.

I went to bed early that evening and was very ill in the night. In the morning there was nothing for it but to see a doctor. The first course of tablets had little effect, and two days later, I asked for some tests to be carried out. The results came back positive for the parasite Giardia intestinalis, and now the cause had been identified, a stronger dose of antibiotics was prescribed. Metronidazole pills are a blessing and a curse. They are effective at targeting the problem, but the side effects are headaches, aching muscles and joints, tiredness, nausea and more. I seemed to be afflicted by them all, and it felt many times as if the cure was as bad as the illness.

Throughout my stay, Peter treated me like one of the family. He and his wife Alice gave me the space I needed to spend time on my own, with no pressure to eat food or be sociable. I couldn't have asked for a more relaxed environment in which to recover.

One very different foodstuff I tasted at Peter's house was durian fruit – I had told him in our email correspondence that I was keen to try it. I knew it had a reputation for smelling so foul that it's banned from buses in Singapore and I'd seen posters in hotels stating that guests are not allowed to bring it into their rooms. Peter told me it was known in Malaysia as the King of

Fruits, but also as the Heaven and Hell Fruit, because 'it tastes like heaven and smells like hell'. He had one of the fruits waiting for me when I arrived, and after tasting it, I can say it deserves its reputation.

On my good days, Peter showed me the sights of the city. The cavernous Batu Cave in the centre of Kuala Lumpur is one of the most popular Hindu sites outside India. At the bottom of the 272 steps leading up to the entrance is the 140-foot statue of Lord Murugan, to whom the cave is dedicated. Once you've climbed the steps and reached the entrance, more steps lead down into a vast cathedral-like cavern, housing Hindu shrines and temples. At the far end where sunlight enters, monkeys run wild, scavenging food from the visitors.

Next to the Batu Cave is the Dark Cave. This doesn't draw so many people as there is an entrance fee, and I was taken round by a guide, courtesy of Peter. It's not called the Dark Cave for nothing. There is no electric lighting and the concrete path through the cave was covered in a carpet of cockroaches, which rattled as they scurried away from the beams of our torches. Hundreds of fruit bats, nectar bats and insect-eating bats inhabit the upper recesses and rats ran into the darkness. Three ghostly cave racer snakes, each around six feet long, slithered along in the gloom. It is a fascinating location for the natural history lover.

On Sunday, Peter and I took our bicycles to Putrajaya. Known as an 'Intelligent Garden City' on the outskirts of Kuala Lumpur, it extends over almost 5000 hectares. The land was originally covered in palm plantations and has been landscaped with elegant and tasteful architecture. Modern administrative buildings, mosques, lakes and bridges blend harmoniously with the traditional styles of Islam. We spent the day cycling round the lakes and parks, returning via the main thoroughfare.

Back at the house, we were discussing my trip and I mentioned that Val and Merv, the couple I met in Turkey and Iran would be in Kuala Lumpur on 16th February. Peter's enthusiasm to host cyclists seemed to have no bounds and it was arranged that they too would stay with him. I expected to be moving on before then, but their arrival date approached and I was still feeling unwell. Peter wouldn't hear of me leaving until I was fully recovered and moved me into his tiny office to free up the twin guest room. I had to admit that I was thrilled at the prospect of meeting my friends again.

Staying longer meant that I would be lucky enough to share the Chinese New Year celebrations in Peter's family home, starting on the 14th of February. On the afternoon of Chinese New Year's Eve, we were at a family get-together when I had a 'bad turn' and had to retire to a darkened room to lie down. I was most embarrassed, but everyone was understanding and couldn't have been more sympathetic. That night, back at Peter's, the meal was a Chinese 'steamboat', a heated pan of anchovy stock, in which shellfish and longevity noodles are dipped and fished out. These extra-long noodles are served traditionally at Chinese New Year's feasts. An ancient Chinese belief holds that long noodles are the key to a long life. I only managed a few shrimps and noodles but I enjoyed being embraced into the family gathering.

Val and Merv arrived in Kuala Lumpur from Chennai and Peter picked them up at the airport. We were thrilled to see each other and spent a lot of time catching up and exchanging stories. Incredibly, they had spent ten weeks in India, eating the food and drinking the water with no ill effects at all. They must have iron constitutions.

Peter continued to be the perfect host, running the three of us around the city to see the sights and taking us to visit his friends and family as part of the New Year festivities.

A week later, we drove to the coast to drop Val and Merv off for the next leg of their journey to Australia, via Singapore and Indonesia. I was sad to say goodbye and once more we vowed to meet again.

For my last sightseeing trip, Peter took me to the island of Pulau Ketam, off the coast of Port Klang (isn't that a fantastic name for a town? Makes you want to put an exclamation mark after it). We caught a packed ferry and disembarked to wind our way round the fishing village of houses built on stilts. We were on foot, but the inhabitants travel around the wooden walkways on bicycles. We didn't see much fishing activity, but watching mudskippers fighting provided endless entertainment. After lunch, we returned to the mainland where we crossed onto Carey Island to see the aboriginal Mah Meri tribe of woodcarvers eking out a living carving souvenirs for tourists.

My last celebration with Peter's family was on the seventh day of Chinese New Year, when we ate Yee Sang or 'Prosperity Toss'. Various shredded raw vegetables are combined on a large plate and overlaid with sauces and strips of salmon. I joined the others standing round the table to toss the ingredients into the air saying "lo hei, lo hei" meaning 'scoop it up'. The height of the food is meant to indicate the growth of the diner's good fortune, and the meal is an important tradition for Chinese living in Singapore and Malaysia. As well as delicious, it was all good fun and I was happy to be included.

Morning came and Peter, Alice and I prepared to leave the city by car to a point where they would drop me off. Two of their sons came with us to say goodbye and as always, Yati the maid was there to close the gates as we left. We drove to Kapar and unloaded my belongings. I'd spent a whole month with this family and could only hope they would make it to England one day so that I could repay them for their kindness. I waved another sad goodbye and with legs feeling quite wobbly, cycled off.

I was hoping to keep my mileage down on that first day but I didn't find lodgings for forty-one miles. I checked in, showered and slept for an hour before venturing out for dinner and vowing to definitely have a short day tomorrow.

One of the many things I learned from Peter (and he is a mine of local information) is that there are three types of weather in Malaysia – hot, very hot and freakin' hot! He told me it was 'freakin' hot time and, if at all possible, to avoid cycling in the afternoon. That's easier said than done because what do you for those four or five hours when the sun is at full height? I didn't rush to get up because the next town of Sabak Bernam was only twenty miles away and I was determined not to go any further. The mileage was plenty for me, and with the help of a local lady I found a lovely Malaysian resort beside the river.

Further north, the prospect of a fifty mile ride from Teluk Intan to Parit filled me with a good deal of anxiety and there was no alternative option. The night before, I set my alarm for 5.30am. After breakfast, I went out into the blackness of the morning with lights on, front and back. Even at that time, the air was warm and humid and the roads were full of commuters travelling the opposite way into town. To my delight, I was rewarded for an early start with the sight of a hornbill as big as a turkey, hopping around an empty bus stop across the road. I desperately tried to capture it on camera but the humidity caused my lens to steam over. In the end, I did the right thing and just enjoyed watching it.

Even though I had a cooling breeze in my face, my clothes were damp against my skin as I cycled. Forty-five miles later, I reached Parit. It was only one o'clock, but the sun was high in the sky and I was ready to find a cool place to stop. I asked a local if he knew of a hotel and he led me round in his car to the only accommodation in town, a Malaysian guesthouse.

A formidable manageress met me in reception with the news that there were no rooms, as the place was closed for maintenance. I protested strongly, saying that the only accommodation in town should not be closed. I'd cycled sixty kilometres and it was too hot to cycle any further. The manageress and her staff retired to an office to deliberate. After a while, I was told there was a room and I could stay. I don't know what I'd have done otherwise – maybe spent a sweaty night in my tent, fending off monkeys.

If you read about cycling in Malaysia, chances are you'll come across the legendary David, who gets a mention in the *Lonely Planet Guide*. David took up cycling for health reasons and then decided to take cyclists into his home and show them the local sights. Anyone who passes his way on a bicycle tour is welcome to stay for a small fee and he is often known to track unsuspecting cyclists down, when one of his local spies in nearby shops and gas stations has alerted him to their presence in the area. In my case, I had contacted him.

David 'takes no prisoners' as they say, and my stay with him kicked off as soon as we met. My bike was lifted into the back of a car and we drove to a coconut plantation to join the workers for their evening meal at the end of the day. Chris and Catherine, two Americans studying in Hong Kong, were already there and the 'toddy wine' or fermented coconut juice, was flowing freely. Our dinner consisted of monitor lizard and goat, served with rice. The food was very tasty but I can't say the same about the toddy. Happily, there was a bottled-beer alternative. At the end of the night, one of the well-soused lumber workers drove us to David's house, with our three bikes in the back of his truck.

The next morning began with a breakfast of pancakes and boiled eggs (fully boiled), on the shady porch outside, and then we piled into David's 4x4 and headed for Penang Island.

Somehow – and I'm still not sure how, I found myself on a 10th-anniversary Hash Harriers run in the afternoon. I'm quite sure I said I didn't want to participate but still found myself trekking through the Malaysian jungle for an hour and a half. Like many others, there was no running on my part.

I had a quiet day the next day, and in the evening, Catherine and I were taken by David to watch cave swiftlets coming in to roost. This is the bird whose nest is so prized by the Chinese for making soup. The birds naturally live in caves, but are farmed in large buildings, where they are encouraged to nest in their hundreds. In the owner's house, we were shown a box of nests ready for sale to the soup market. Each cupped nest made of bird spittle was worth more than gold by weight.

There was more to come when David took us for a sail down the river to watch fireflies. I had a magical moment when one of the boatmen scooped some of the insects up in a net and I was able to hold one in the palm of my hand, with the glow of its body pulsating in the dark. I left David's with a wealth of new experiences under my belt.

Once more on my own, cycling north and travelling through more palm plantations, I noticed a tall termite mound with a hole in the top, and stopped to investigate. As I parked my bike, a car pulled up and a small Malaysian man who looked as if he might work on the plantations, got out and asked me where I was going. When I told him about my journey he asked me for some "pearls of wisdom". It seemed like an unusual request and I was stumped for an answer at first. After giving it some more thought, I said "Don't let life pass you by" and then, thinking again said, "Don't believe everything you hear. People round the world are good". He seemed quite happy with this and then, to my surprise, took out a ten ringgit note and asked me to accept it as a gift. I was touched and could tell he wanted me to have it, so I gracefully accepted. He drove off into the distance and I carried on cycling. Three miles further down the road, there he was again, and this time he took out a small amethyst ring and what I thought was a five ringgit note. He was obviously determined to leave me with something more to remember him by, and although it was becoming a little embarrassing, I again accepted. When I asked him his name, he said, "Just call me Mr Termite". It wasn't until later, that I saw the last note he gave me was a fifty ringgit note.

I was sailing to Thailand via Langkawi Island, and after a late breakfast on the mainland, I rode seven miles to the ferry and arrived on the island at 3pm. The ferry crossing had been straightforward enough. There was little to distract me, other than a bad movie with incomprehensible English subtitles, obviously software-generated, and the odd cockroach running around the seats, sometimes even on the passengers themselves. I spent a night on Langkawi Island and caught another ferry to Satun at the southern tip of Thailand.

Thailand

Crabby in Krabi

It was seven miles from the harbour to Satun, a small town with two hotels and a restaurant which served a few western dishes. My last meal in Malaysia was Thai green curry, and the first meal I had in Thailand was chicken and mushroom pie with chips, salad AND... HP sauce – heaven!

I left Satun early to cycle to Thung Wa, a distance of forty-four miles. The scenery was changing from palm to rubber plantations, and people were just as friendly as in Malaysia, but now with the surprised expression on their faces that had been pleasantly absent in Malaysia. I breakfasted on pad thai at a roadside café and was delighted to find packets of my favourite food, chestnuts.

On a rubber-tree-lined road, I pulled into the shade for a rest, and it wasn't long before a local man on a motorbike stopped to talk to me. With his workman's clothes, rubber boots and one eye, I guessed he was a forestry worker. He spoke not a word of English, but this didn't stop him from babbling on as I shook my head and shrugged my shoulders. Whatever he said seemed to please him and he moved on.

On the road to Trang, I bumped into another touring cyclist from Belgium. Hugo was forty and a seasoned traveller. He was very fair skinned and sported a white Legionnaire hat for maximum sun protection. His English was perfect and we had a long chat over cold drinks, exchanging stories of the road. He'd been travelling for six years and had toured countless countries, but he was still surprised to meet a woman of my age on the road. "What's it like to be sixty?" he asked. "I don't know", I said – "it doesn't feel much different to forty. It's just a number." We talked about the road north, and he advised me to backtrack ten kilometres to Pak Meng beach to find a resort.

In Pak Meng, I weighed up the next leg to Krabi, over sixty-five miles away. I still hadn't regained my strength and there was no guarantee of finding somewhere in between, so I took a day off to get a good rest. I also had a sneaking feeling I had a cold coming on.

After a late start, I reached Krabi around lunchtime, by which time my cold was full-blown. The hotel room was dismal – too small, a miserable excuse for a window with a brick wall for a view, and inefficient air-con. Trying my best to convince myself that I'd be past the worst of the cold by morning, I booked an island tour round the coast. I reckoned I'd be better out relaxing in the fresh air, than cooped up inside.

Krabi itself did nothing to lift my spirits. The guide books tell you it's mainly a stopping off point for people heading to the more exotic islands and resorts that line the coast of the Andaman Sea. The town centre had little to commend it, other than a set of incredible traffic light sculptures atop poles. The best way I can describe them is to say they are in the shape of prehistoric cavemen holding suitcases. In the rectangular ends of the suitcases, the regulated coloured lights shine towards the traffic. They were extremely ugly but at the same time, extremely funny.

The boat trip was a good decision overall, but I did wish I'd been in a better state to enjoy the day. We sailed past a floating village, much like the ones I'd seen in Malaysia and then on to 'James Bond Island', where scenes from The Man with the Golden Gun had been shot. The boat brought us back to the floating village for lunch and then onto a Buddhist temple within a cave, much like the Batu Cave in Malaysia, only smaller.

The next day I slept until well past check-out time and had no choice but to pay for a third night. The following morning I was still groggy but couldn't stand another night in that room, so I set off around 10am thinking I would move on and make it a short day. Less than four miles along the road out of town, I stopped in the shade of a shed. I was covered in sweat, shaking all over and downed all my water supply in one go. Temperatures were in the high thirties and in my state, it was obvious I wasn't going anywhere. I cycled back to Krabi where I booked into a much nicer hotel with a large room, a large window overlooking treetops and good air-con.

Looking at maps and distances, I reassessed the situation and altered my plans. I would cut across to the east coast of Thailand and go by train to Cambodia, via Bangkok. This would serve more than one purpose; firstly, my rate of progress had been so slow that life on the road was beginning to lose its charm. It was taking me all day to cycle thirty miles and then I was shattered. It was too hot to go outside in the afternoon, so I spent most of my time inside. Secondly, after losing a month in Kuala Lumpur and another week in Krabi, I'd slipped well behind schedule again, with regard to the coming months. It now looked as though I would be able to cross the United States, but I needed to be sure of reaching the eastern side before the American winter set in. Thirdly, I was about to enter Cambodia, in what I'd read described as 'the killer month of April, where temperatures can reach 40 degrees'. To wait any longer, would take me into the monsoon period. I nursed my cold until I was ready to move on.

Three days later and now in Thap Phut, I was directed to the only accommodation – one of the establishments that sometimes has '24' written on the board outside, but usually the number is in Thai. Hugo, the Belgian cyclist had informed me that these places were basically sex hotels, but I'd already stopped in one by then and if there's no alternative and you feel safe, which I did, what do you do? At 350 bahts it was a bargain and perfectly clean, even if the horizontal mirror beside the bed was a little distracting.

I bought my overnight train ticket in Surat Thani and went to look for lunch. The streets were full of stalls where vendors fried seafood and stirred tureens of food which they sold in plastic bags. In the park where I took my 'takeaway', people were exercising and relaxing. Adults jogged and cycled around the perimeter and young men played football. Groups of children sat on the ground painting models and others played on swings and ropes. It was a pleasant scene to entertain me until my train left.

I arrived in Bangkok the following day after a reasonably good night's sleep. From the next train to the border town of Aranyaprathet I watched the land levelling out into marshy wetlands. Water stood in ditches and ponds, cranes, herons and egrets populated the landscape, and ploughed fields stretched out into the distance, separated by dirt roads of red sand. The scenery was typical of the floodplain of southern Cambodia, and the waterlogged fields were a good sign, because it meant that the boat from Battambang to Siem Reap across the Tonle Sap was still running.

The border town of Poipet is known to tourists as Hustle Central, a nightmare of markets, casinos and hawkers trying to persuade you to purchase a visa through them. Ignoring all advances, I entered the passport control office with Sofi and managed to get to the counter before I was told by an official that I must take my bike outside. I remonstrated as much as I could get away with, but in the packed hall it was difficult not to see his point and I wheeled the bike outside. Fortunately, I was allowed back to the front of the queue, so that Sofi wasn't left unguarded for very long.

In the visa office, five uniformed men lounged idly in their chairs and one of them took my money saying I was very beautiful. 'Yes', I thought 'and you think I'm a rich westerner.'

Cambodia

An Unexpected Dip

The difference between Thailand and Cambodia was apparent as soon as I'd passed through the last checkpoint. Cambodia was much poorer than Thailand. Both countries had roadside stalls, but here, they had comparatively little to sell. There were no Coca Cola, Pepsi or Wall's ice cream signs to be seen. Along the road behind me, a steady stream of Cambodians were pulling wooden handcarts into Thailand to load up with goods that weren't available in their own country.

This was my second visit to Cambodia, so it was no surprise to feel the warmth and gentleness of the people here. I reached Sisophon and checked into the Golden Crown Guest House, a cheap and cheerful hotel which promised wi-fi, but the connection was poor; the hot shower was a bonus however. While I was soothing my aching knees in the warmth of the running water, I discovered a number of small bites covering my ribs. Something in Thailand had obviously feasted on me.

There was a busy market close to the hotel and I wandered outside to look round. Stalls of raw meat buzzed with flies and fish gaped for air in shallow bowls of water. One woman stood a live fish on end, nose down, while she sliced off the fins. I just wished she'd taken the head off first; it would have been a quicker ending for the fish. Motorbikes whizzed past with live pigs strapped on the back in cane cages, each of which had a tapered end to accommodate the animal's head. In spite of my concerns about animal welfare, I slept well and cycled to the next town.

Battambang, that drumbeat of a name, brought back memories of watching UK news correspondents reporting from the town in the 70's. Thousands of Cambodians walked hundreds of miles through the country, crossing to the safety of Thailand to escape the regime of the madman Pol Pot and his brutal Khmer Rouge army. On my ride to the town, I saw orderly ploughed fields and wondered what the picture would have looked like between 1975 and 1979 when the whole population was forced into agricultural work on ill-thought-out schemes that inevitably foundered. Now Battambang is a peaceful place with cheerful inhabitants. Its French colonial history can be seen in the architecture and layout of the roads.

The manageress of the first hotel told me that the ferry to Siem Reap wasn't running because of the low water level. Her English wasn't good and we were struggling to communicate. The heat was affecting my tolerance levels and I gave up and went to another hotel. The manager there spoke much better English and told me the boat would be running on Tuesday. It was Sunday now, so I spent two days exploring. Any excuse for a rest was welcome in the heat.

The boat departed at 7am which meant an early rise at 5.45 to get to the port on time for the fascinating journey down the Sangker River and across the Tonle Sap, a lake of central importance to the food provision of the country. The ferry itself was anything but comfortable, but the passengers enjoyed picturesque views of the riverbanks and the life that exists there. A combination of high summer temperatures and the downpours of the monsoons, cause the lake to vary in size throughout the year. The reason for the uncertainty of our sailing was its present low level and there were many anxious moments when the boat threatened to become grounded. Thanks to a skilful driver and his assistant who pushed us off each time, we continued along with no major incidents – until we reached Siem Reap that is.

As we approached the jetty, a group of touts were awaiting our arrival and jumped on the boat as soon as it docked, each choosing one of us as a target. Some even had our names written on large pieces of paper, which they'd presumably acquired from the registration list. I rarely have any trouble with touts because I refuse to engage with them and if you give a firm 'no', they will move to an easier 'victim' (or maybe I've just become scary in my old age). My conversation with one of them went like this:

"You want a hotel?"

"No thank you."

"I will take you there."

"I have a bicycle. I will take myself."

"But it's not safe."

"I think it is."

"So you don't care about your children?"

"No – I don't care about my children" (sorry kids – it WAS a silly question.)

That remark must have offended some higher being (or maybe my children heard me?) because with one hand firmly on a pole on the side of the boat, I stepped onto the jetty and immediately slipped off with a splash! into the lake. As I fell, I made a grab for the pole with my other hand and luckily only went in waist deep. My greatest concern at that point was my bar-bag around my neck. It had everything of value in it – passport, money, camera, specs. Fortunately, when the bag hit the water, it lived up to the manufacturer's claim of being totally waterproof, and did exactly what it was supposed to do – it floated.

While I was hanging there, one of the passengers took my bag, while the touts, who were stifling their laughter in front of the punters, helped haul me out. I was most disconcerted at just how difficult that was, considering all the weight I'd lost.

I clambered onto the jetty and of course, everyone was asking if I was OK. Well, I was OK, if a little damp. The lake water was quite warm and not an unpleasant experience. I remember saying something about damaged dignity, but afterwards thought to myself 'Why did I say that?? I've been stared at for the last nine months, sometimes gathering a crowd just by eating a bag of crisps. I'd performed the 'Great Bike Packing Event' in Kolkata airport – why would getting my lower half wet worry me?' I just wished I'd had a photograph of what happened; it would have been an entertaining souvenir. Maybe the other passengers took some, but if they did, they were too polite to say.

The crowd dispersed as I loaded my bike. Then I scattered a group of cheeky children who wanted to get too close to it, and dragged my soggy *rse onto the saddle. It was just over seven miles to Siem Reap, and by the time I got there, I'd dried out completely.

As I've mentioned, this was my second visit to Cambodia and it was a pleasant surprise to see that a restaurant where I'd dined four years ago was still there – the Dead Fish. The place boasts a menu which declares 'no dog, cat, rat or worm' and has a crocodile pit in the far corner. You can buy food for the crocodiles if you want to prove they are alive.

I had an enjoyable evening, dining on chicken and cashew nuts and probably more glasses of Angkor beer than I should.

The Dead Fish was the first place since leaving home where I recognised my surroundings, and I was enjoying it. It felt very relaxing and comfortable (or was it the alcohol?) Whatever, I wasn't rushing to leave town, especially as I'd found a room for ten dollars a night.

Siem Reap is one of the most special places on earth and it is one of life's greatest pleasures to walk among the ruins of the temples. Angkor Wat is the largest religious monument in the world and the whole complex is recognised as the eighth wonder of the world. For me, the nearby Bayon Temple at Angkor Thom is the most beautiful ruin. It is carved with a multitude of serene and massive stone faces of Buddha on the numerous towers projecting from the upper terrace and clustering around its central peak. Approximately one kilometre east of Angkor Thom lies Ta Promh. It was used in the film 'Tomb Raiders' and the most unreal temple of all. Its crumbling ruins were discovered overgrown with trees and with branches and roots creeping through the stonework. The buildings have been stabilised and the trees left as they are for the benefit of the thousands of tourists who flock to see this strange sight.

There were more tourists, bars and restaurants in Siem Reap than I remembered five years before, but that turned out to be a blessing when I discovered lots of western food on the menus. My insides were still not ready to try adventurous local food. One thing that struck me was that the town looked tidier and the traffic seemed much less frantic than on my previous visit. Was that the case, or had all those miles in India rendered me impervious to the chaos?

The heat was still a problem and I planned to move on to South Korea as soon as possible. The international weather reports on TV showed that the temperature in Seoul was fourteen degrees – a long way from the forty degrees in SE Asia. I spent three days in Siem Reap and then took a bus to Phnom Penh, for some sightseeing before my next flight.

The bus journey to the capital was surprisingly comfortable. Most aspects of Cambodian life are not as advanced as those of other countries, but I had no complaints about the bus. It was a double-decker affair, with passengers on top and numerous small motorbikes, as well as Sofi, stored below with the luggage.

The trip lasted around six hours, broken up with a number of stops along the way. At some of the stops, locals would appear with snacks and drinks to sell. From my upstairs position, I looked down on a basin of goodies carried on the head of a local lady. It was full of large, black, spiders. From their rigid bodies I assumed they were cooked, not unlike the platter of cockroaches I saw in the Siem Reap market. Were these delicacies of choice to the locals, or just another indication of the poverty?

Aside from the palace, the capital Phnom Penh didn't have a great deal to offer, but I wanted to see the genocide museums dedicated to those who perished under Pol Pot and the Khmer Rouge. The main sights could have been seen in one day, but I needed time to book my flight to South Korea and make arrangements for the bike. Three months of intense heat had completely fried my brain, and every job seemed to be more of an effort than it should. Flying with a bike is probably the most stressful part of any trip, so I gave myself a few days in the city to make my arrangements with no pressure. I spent the first day getting my bearings and taking things easy in the sweltering heat.

When I booked my flight to Seoul, I was told that the airline could plastic-wrap the bike. That would make things a whole lot easier in many ways, but I was anxious about Sofi getting damaged. I resolved to take off the handlebars, front wheel and front pannier rack and tape them firmly within the frame area to prevent breakage.

One afternoon I visited Choeung Ek, billed as 'The Killing Fields' for tourists. It seemed rather macabre to be asked by a cheerful driver if I wanted to take a "tuk-tuk to see the Killing

Fields?" but I guess that thirty years on, the populace has to find some way of dealing with a horrific period in their history, which must still impact each and every one.

Choeung Ek was a site used to torture and murder victims and dispose of their bodies in mass graves. The bones have been recovered and are housed in a purpose-built memorial tower to serve as a lasting reminder of the atrocities.

The following day, I visited Toul Sleng or S-21 as it was known from 1975 to 1979. Again, another grisly day out, this time to see the camp where prisoners were interrogated and killed in what had once been a city school.

Close to the palace and on the river front a wide variety of western food was available for the tourist. I could get a 'full English' breakfast, and the bacon was surprisingly good, albeit slightly tainted having seen the way the locals transport pigs.

On April 15th I cycled to the airport and rearranged the bike as planned. Watching Sofi being shrink-wrapped in cling-film on a turntable, with nothing more than thin plastic for protection, I was a lot less than happy and decided that a cardboard box would have been by far the best option.

The Bayon temple at Angkor Thom, Cambodia

The Nek Chand Fantasy Rock Garden, Chandigargh

Arriving frail at Peter's house, Malaysia

YHA staff in Kolkata

With Peter, Val and Merv at Putra Jaya

David, Malaysia

Part Three

The F.U.N. is Back!

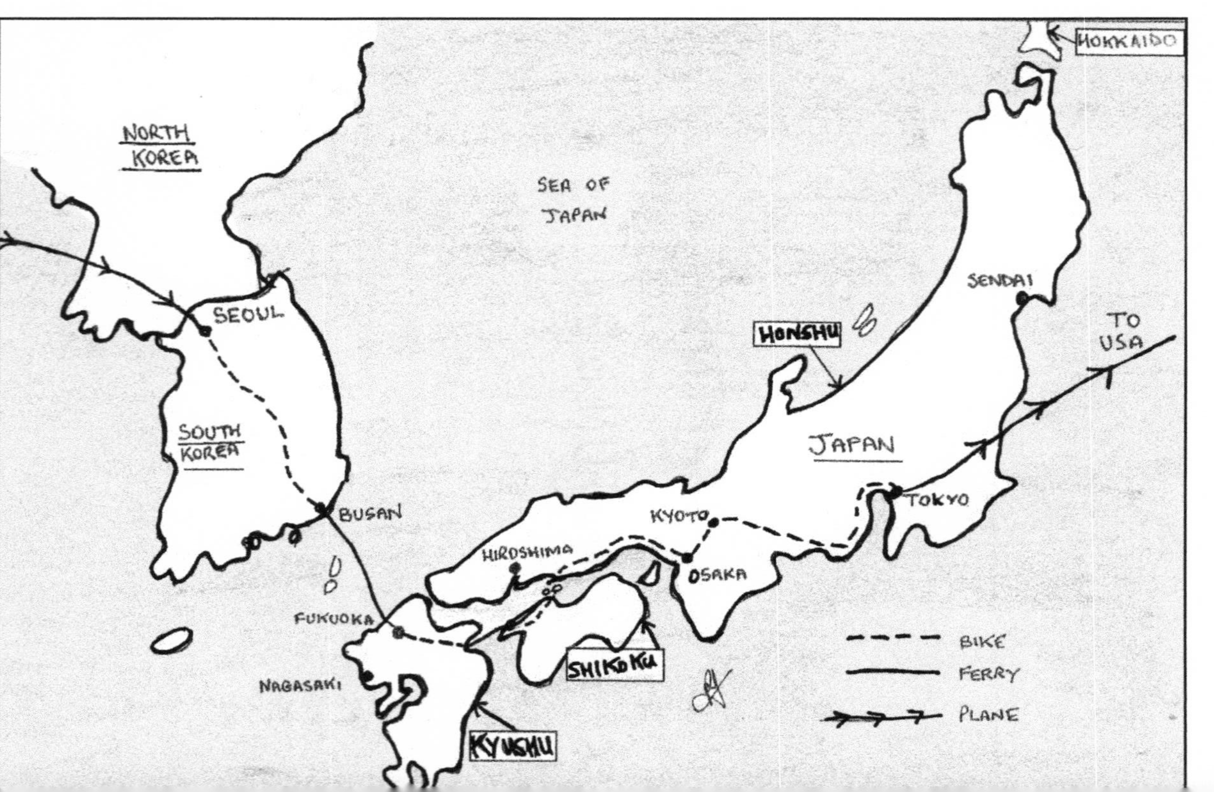
HOKKAIDO
NORTH KOREA
SEA OF JAPAN
SEOUL
HONSHU
SENDAI
TO USA
SOUTH KOREA
JAPAN
TOKYO
BUSAN
KYOTO
HIROSHIMA
OSAKA
FUKUOKA
BIKE
FERRY
SHIKOKU
NAGASAKI
PLANE
KYUSHU

South Korea

The F.U.N. is back!

Seoul-Incheon International Airport lies on an artificially created piece of land thirty kilometres to the west of the capital, and is connected to the mainland by Incheon International Airport Expressway. Sofi and I arrived around 7am South Korean time and I found a quiet corner to re-assemble the (thankfully-undamaged) bike and re-organise my panniers. With my life in order and a breakfast of coffee and a scone inside me, I headed for the train to the city centre. As usual, I could feel all eyes on me as I wheeled the loaded bike through arrivals and it wasn't long before a young man stopped to ask about my journey. I recounted my story, and as expected, he showed great interest and told me how impressed he was. It was reassuring to encounter such friendliness and when he took out a small multi-tool penknife and offered it to me as a gift, I thanked him kindly. I was beginning to get used to such reactions and found it best to accept graciously.

I left the spotless train at Gimpo station on the south side of the River Han and trundled off towards the city centre, which appeared to be on the north side. As well as a needing a hotel, I wanted to find a map and arrange a trip to the Demilitarised Zone (known by its abbreviation DMZ) between North and South Korea. The hotels I tried were much too expensive, so it was plan B – go back to the south side of the river where accommodation may be a little cheaper. Here, the traffic was a cyclist's nightmare, with rows of filtering lanes leading off in all directions. My aim was to pick up the riverside cycle path to my left, but it was impossible to cross the rows of cars and I found myself being channelled to the right. The area I ended up in was just as expensive, and I later discovered that there is no real centre to Seoul. Like many capital cities, it is a sprawling metropolis with a number of districts, each with its own commercial centre.

It was becoming clear that few people spoke English, and unusually, hotel staff were no exception. Booking a room was a struggle and asking about a trip to the DMZ brought forth blank looks. Should I persevere or just head out south on my chosen route to Busan? What with the language barrier and the limited number of signs in English, seeing the DMZ seemed like an impossible task. The next morning, I walked into town to buy a city map and plan my exit. In the busy streets, an American directed me to a bookshop, but it didn't sell maps of the city, so I went for a coffee.

The café was a typically stylish city eatery, packed with fashionable young people chattering away. Feeling severely under-dressed and out of place, I finished my pizza and set out to try and make some sense of the Korean street signs. I'd only walked a few yards when I was approached by a charming young woman, who had seen me in the café and followed me out. Yu-jin was an environmental scientist studying global warming. She was flying to Germany the next day to give a presentation and wanted to talk to me to practise her English. This was a golden opportunity for us both and we went to another quieter café, where she helped me book a trip to the DMZ for the next day.

In South East Asia, where temperatures had touched forty degrees, I had left some of my warmer clothing with Peter's maid Yati. Now, in South Korea, it was more like fourteen degrees and I arrived at the pickup point wearing as many layers as I could muster. By the time we arrived at the DMZ, I had started shivering, so I dived into the souvenir shop to grab something to wear to avoid galloping hypothermia. I came out with a rather nice hoodie with DMZ in bold white letters on the front.

It was an interesting morning which brought home the political strains such nations are living with, while we in the west have comparatively few worries from our neighbours. The zone is a strip of land running across the Korean peninsula and dividing South from North. Its name alone is a contradiction because it is the most militarised border in the world. Large numbers of troops are stationed on both sides, each guarding against potential aggression from the other. As tourists, we were very much aware that our movements were being closely observed. Miles of razor wire, stretching east and west, gave us a chilling reminder of the hostilities and the sad history of family divisions which have remained since the end of the Korean War.

Back in the city centre, I went down to the subway to find a train back to my hotel. While I was looking at maps and being helped by the underground staff who spoke little or no English, who should appear but Yu-jin. Her flight had been cancelled because of the Iceland volcano eruption and she'd come looking for me. I was astonished that she found me.

We had lunch together before visiting a part of the old town which had a craft fair and art galleries, and finally, my new friend escorted me to my hotel on the bus. Yu-jin had once again made life very easy for me.

I left the city the next morning and headed out in a light shower to find the River Han bike-path. Within a few days, the FUN was back in cycling! With temperatures so much cooler, I felt stronger than I had for a long time. Whilst I'd been recovering from my illness in South East Asia, the heat had completely floored me and it was difficult to judge whether I would even cope under temperate conditions. There were times when I wondered if I'd run out of steam altogether. Soon, my doubts disappeared. With so many hours in the day to cycle and no racing to get indoors out of the baking sun, the pressure was off. I could lie in until 9am if I wanted and still have enough time to get a reasonable number of miles under my wheels.

My route to Busan was one I came across while I was in Kuala Lumpur reading another cycling journal. A set of free maps, created by a Dutch cyclist, take you from Seoul to Busan over the mountainous spine of the country, along riversides and quiet roads. Distances and accommodation were included and the information made travelling very easy for someone who had been using guesswork up to now. It felt almost like a holiday within my trip. Conditions were ideal and my days became thoroughly enjoyable. It was early spring in the north of the country and the land was awakening from winter. Trees were mainly bare, but winter jasmine and that favourite of the east, cherry blossom abounded. The roads were good and drivers considerate. Korean people are either extremely polite or extremely shy and tend to look away as you approach. I had no pips from vehicles and only a handful of waves and shouts.

I left Suanbo on Thursday for a day that would take me over the highest point on the route, the Ihwaryeong Pass at 524m. After all my puffing and panting, the panoramic views of the valley below made it all worth the effort. South Korea has a paucity of farming land, as most of the country is mountainous, and down on the river floor you could now see that every inch of land was utilised to produce crops, the most important of which is rice. Another valuable crop is ginseng, and the black-shaded housing, like giant packs of cards, can be seen dotted around the landscape. I reached the summit of the pass, and went into the gift shop. I was hoping to find food but the restaurant was closed. A group of people came out of the shop to look at Sofi and drool excitedly over my maps. On parting I was once again the recipient of a gift, when they left me with a large orange for my larder.

From the highpoint, a soaring downhill took me to the edge of the Mungyeong National Park and to a restaurant. I ordered from the menu using lots of pointing and nodding. I hardly knew what to expect and was faced with a meal of soup, fish, nuts and leaves, to be eaten with the metal chopsticks which distinguish the culture. I counted twelve small plates on the table – lots of work for 'washer uppers'.

A few hops along the side of the main highway took me to an old road beside a slow flowing river and a disused railway line. A final crossing of the river and I was on a quiet cycle path leading to a motel in Sangui.

My son, who lives in Tokyo, explained that what are known as Love Hotels are generally fairly respectable establishments in this part of the world. They exist to provide private rooms for married couples who share accommodation with their parents. Family apartments are normally very small by western standards and have paper thin walls, giving the young couples very little privacy for marital intimacy. Their only chance to escape this disadvantage of communal living is to take a room in a Love Hotel for a few hours of unbridled passion.

When I turned on the lights in my room, its purpose was fairly obvious. Red lights illuminated the side of the headboard and shone from under the bed. There was a massive TV screen in the room and the widest variety of 'freebies' on the dressing table I'd ever seen, including condoms and lubricant. Security was hi-tech and customers didn't need a key because the room door was locked remotely from reception. I felt perfectly safe.

When I woke to a grisly, foggy day the next morning, I was very tempted to stay another night, but the morning wore on and brightened. It was only twenty-five miles to the next hostelry, so at lunchtime I packed and left.

I was so glad I had because by afternoon I was trundling along country roads through farms and villages, on deserted lanes among delightful scenery. Cherry trees covered in clouds of pink blossom lined the roads; fields full of black net canopies covered ginseng crops; orderly rows of vegetables were obscured with lines of black plastic, and any waste was neatly packed in bins on the roadsides. Men and women worked industriously harvesting vegetables, their heads shaded from the sun with wide-brimmed hats and neckerchiefs.

After taking my time to enjoy the ride, I arrived in Gudam around 4pm. Just as I reached a motel, I was stopped by a young man who jumped out of his truck to insist in very loud broken English that I must stay with him instead of spending money. 'I've been here before' I thought, but this time there was no-one to vouch for him. When I politely but firmly declined his offer, he still insisted on helping and led me to the motel where he translated my requirements to the manager. It's a pity the circumstances hadn't been slightly different, as I'm sure his intentions were honourable. I probably missed the chance of a cultural experience with locals.

Although eating in restaurants was a challenge, daytime food was simple. In most motels there were drinks units that dispensed both boiling and chilled water. In the convenience stores, I found a snack called Jolly Pong which is exactly the same as one of our British cereals, Sugar Puffs. Fresh milk was available everywhere, so I had cereal and fruit for breakfast with a hot drink, and for lunch, I bought Gimpa, a delicious boiled rice snack wrapped in seaweed. It comes in small plastic packets and must be opened in a certain way, otherwise you'll be left with a pile of soggy rice in your hands. With breakfast and lunch sorted I could cycle for hours and there was no doubt that my fitness level was improving.

In the village of Sannae I found myself a room and went out for the nightly challenge of food charades. In the first restaurant, I just wasn't getting anywhere – the waiter spoke no English and there were no pictures on the menu. In desperation, I asked a group of diners if anyone spoke English. They shook their heads in a good-natured way and then one of them beckoned to me.

He escorted me across the road to another restaurant, ordered me a meal and left. Obediently I sat down on the floor and waited to see what turned up. Once again, it was a crockery frenzy of soup and rice with seven or eight side dishes. The soup had suspicious looking grey things in it, but on close examination, they turned out to be tiny periwinkles. That was fine, at least it wasn't spicy and I could choose which of the side dishes I wanted. Overall, it was very good.

A young man and his elderly mother entered the restaurant after me and they finished their meal about the same time as I did. Surprisingly, for this remote part of the country, the young man spoke excellent English and came over to talk. He was wondering what I was doing in such a remote area, so I explained. Before long, I had told him all about the countries I had visited. At the end of our conversation he asked me if I would do him a favour and allow him to pay for my meal. How could I refuse such a request? What a delightful man.

My health was improving dramatically, as was my daily mileage. Further south there was another steep hill to climb and as I approached the summit it started to rain. I could see from my map that there was a ten-kilometre downhill coming up, so I put on my waterproofs and pushed to the top. A long descent took me within sight of Eon Yang, one of the ugliest towns I'd seen – huge escarpments of high-rise flats everywhere. I had thought of staying there but it looked so depressing in the rain that I decided to bypass it. This was not to be however, because where there should have been a sign to take me around the town, a new piece of road was being laid and the sign was missing. I was heading towards the town centre and by now I was soaked. I began to look out for a motel; one here, none there and then four in a cluster – each one as depressing as the next. In one, the reception desk was no more than a hatch looking into a tiny room occupied by a young woman and her children. It was sad to see the family imprisoned in such a confined space. The last of the four was located above business premises and I pushed open the door with little optimism. Through the hatch and in the room behind, I could see a man lying prostrate on the floor with legs akimbo and snoring. His mouth was wide open showing a row of gold teeth. I tentatively knocked but I wasn't sorry when he didn't wake. It was time to look elsewhere. I cycled off and spotted the '35' road I needed. The next motel on the map couldn't be any worse.

Back on the road everything was going comparatively well until I remembered that the next village I was looking out for also went by the name of the local temple Tongdo-sa. Just as the thought struck me, I spotted the name on a sign, took a sharp right off the 35 and, with an ominously huge circular sweep, the road delivered me to the toll plaza of Expressway 1 – not a good place to be on a bicycle. I was trying to work out the best way out of my predicament when the lady toll guard frantically stopped me in my tracks and told me to wait. Great! – wet through and cold, on a bicycle and stuck on an Expressway. During lulls between trucks passing her tollbooth, she tried to persuade me to go down a steep muddy embankment to the road below. I was having none of that because I could see I'd end up filthy as well as wet. Finally, a young man appeared like a meerkat from an underground chamber below the road, and carried my bike and bags down the banking. Back on track, I followed his instructions and arrived in Tongdo-sa, where there were motels everywhere. I checked in to the first and had a hot bath before venturing outside for a meal, this time chosen from pictures on the menu. Not the best of days but it turned out alright in the end.

Busan is the second most populous city in South Korea, but getting close to the centre was relatively painless. My maps guided me in through the north of the conurbation and I had the pleasure of riding cycle paths in the countryside, while watching cars fighting for space on the highways in the distance.

My brakes were beginning to feel 'mushy', and on inspection it was clear that the brake pads needed replacing. I didn't want to enter Japan with the bike needing attention, so I stopped at the first bicycle repair shop. Even with the language barrier the owner was more than helpful. He replaced the front and back pads, pumped up the back tyre and gave me coffee and a bun while he worked.

My time in South Korea was coming to an end and I'd been looking forward to reaching Japan since being in India. The thought of visiting my son Matthew in Tokyo had kept me going on those miserable days when I felt ill, but here in South Korea, the task of taking a boat ride to Japan had become a little more daunting. How would I find a boat in a land where so little English was spoken? The challenge was getting nearer, now I was actually in Busan.

Cycling became more difficult nearer the busy city centre, faced as I was with its confusing signs, acres of densely built tower blocks and a population of 3.6 million. The scale of my maps was too small to be of any use and I eventually found my way to the ferry terminal by following signs for the train station. Thankfully, some of the staff there spoke English and pointed me in the right direction.

At the terminal, my bike was refused on the faster daytime ferry and I was forced to take the overnight crossing to Fukuoka, which cost me five times as much but saved me the price of a motel.

Japan
60 Years Young

The ferry docked in Fukuoka on Kyushu, the most southerly of Japan's main islands at 6.30am and passengers disembarked at 7.30am.

The map I picked up at the information desk wasn't much help so I followed buses and taxis towards the city centre. Once away from the terminal, the map began to make more sense. This was my second visit to Japan, and as the town awoke and other cyclists appeared, I remembered I could ride on the pavement – much less stressful than on the road. It was still early and I was in time to see a group of employees doing their traditional morning exercises in the office car park. At one set of traffic lights, I was amused to hear the tune to Robbie Burns' 'Comin' Thro' the Rye' being played as the lights changed to green. I was sure my Scottish friend Val would be tickled pink to hear of it.

At 10am, I was the first customer at the tourist information desk, where I received excellent service and was booked into a hotel for the night. I couldn't check in until 3pm but I could leave my bags there at noon. My arrival in Japan had coincided with the national holiday Golden Week, and accommodation was going to be something of a challenge to find over the next seven days. The tourist office had no road maps in English, so I took the best they had and went for lunch at Starbucks, thinking I might be able to check my mail. It turned out wi-fi wasn't available, but sandwiches and cappuccino were a welcome treat. At midday, I left my bags at the hotel and went for a ride around the local neighbourhood until 3pm. How on earth, I wondered, was I going to find my way out of town when the best map I had was a flimsy one in Japanese?

The hotel room was compact to say the least, but clean and adequate. A kimono dressing gown and slippers were provided, together with toothpaste and toothbrush. Washroom facilities were communal and economically spaced. In the lavatories, two urinals faced the entrance door in which was a small window. Admittedly, a passer-by would only see the backs of any gents using them, but why have a window there in the first place? It was all a mystery to me, but there were times when I would have sold my soul for such luxury in India.

Japan is a fascinating country and many aspects of the culture constantly surprise foreigners like myself. Vending machines can be found on almost every street corner dispensing drinks. They are always spotlessly clean, in full working order and well stocked. Not only that, they give change. Smartly uniformed attendants carrying batons like shortened lightsabres supervise cars in large commercial carparks. Toilets are a wonder of technology. Some have buttons which will heat, spray and dry your nether regions, and for the more modest, play tunes as you go about your business. Politeness and tradition are qualities fundamental to society. One of their colourful festivities, The Boys' Festival (Tango no Sekku), is celebrated on May 5th. Families pray for the health and future success of their sons by hanging up streamers of bright billowing carp outside their houses and displaying samurai dolls, both of which symbolize strength, power and success in life. Japanese food is wide and varied. Don't worry if you don't like raw fish, there are plenty of cooked dishes to choose from. And it doesn't matter if you can't read the menu because many restaurants have plastic models of the dishes in their windows. These sampuru are so realistic, that the craftsmanship has been raised to an art form. One of the times of year most popular with the Japanese, is during the cherry blossom season, when parks are filled with promenaders enjoying the beauty of the flowers. I don't think I could ever tire of this country.

The next morning, I set out through the high rise buildings and intimidating fly-overs to find highway number three. It didn't take long and I was able to stay on pavements for around twenty miles, apart from a couple of dangerous interchanges, which I might have avoided had I been able to read the signs.

The ride was going well until I reached a tunnel. I walked my way through it, only to see another one 200m further on. At that point, the pathway on the opposite side was much wider, so I waited for a gap in the traffic and crossed. Things didn't improve at the end of the tunnel because there was no hard shoulder and I had to compete with the cars. By the time I reached Kurosaki, I was ready to get off the road and call it a day.

I continued on the same road the next day, but after a couple of miles another tunnel loomed into view with a ban on cyclists. 'Maybe I shouldn't be on the road in the first place' I wondered. I took off to the left to see if there was any obvious detour but found myself totally confused by signs and at a loss for a plan. There was nothing for it but to turn round, and ride back into the town I'd just left to find a better map, be it in English or Japanese. An hour later and equipped with the clearest Japanese map available, I set off again. What a difference – it was amazing how well I could cope now using the road numbers, even if I couldn't read the town names. I was soon on the '51', riding on pavements through quieter urban areas with no problems.

In the warm afternoon sun, I felt as if I could ride forever. I had romantic notions of pitching my tent on a secluded grassy patch and sleeping in the fresh air, but as the evening drew on and temperatures dropped I abandoned that idea and found a hotel in Nakatsu.

Japan is made up of many islands, the four largest of which are Kyushu (where I arrived), Shikoku, Honshu and Hokkaido. I was heading to Tokyo, on Honshu, and would first need to take a ferry to Shikoku. After crossing Shikoku, I would follow the Shimanami Kaido sea-bridge route, a sixty-kilometre-long toll road, which connects Shikoku with the main island Honshu, and passes over six smaller islands in the Seto Inland Sea. I'd seen aerial photographs of the road leapfrogging over the islands and was looking forward to cycling it.

Beppu sits on the side of a picturesque bay and boasts hot springs and onsens (steam baths). I was hoping to sail from there to Matsuyama on Shikoku, but because of the national holiday, the only seat available was on a boat to Yawatahama, forty-five miles further south. As it would be three days before I could sail to Matsuyama, and finding a room in Beppu while I waited would be difficult in Golden Week, I needed a change of plan. I booked a passage to Yawatahama, where I spent the night in a guest house and enjoyed a tasty, if somewhat strange, breakfast of poached egg with lettuce and strawberries. The road from Yawatahama passed through four tunnels, but after that the journey was plain sailing and I had a great ride along a quiet road which hugged the coast all the way.

I found a hotel in Matsuyama close to the station and checked in. In the process of giving my details and parking my bike, I'd somehow omitted to pay for the room. This resulted in a scenario of comedic proportions when the staff tried to explain to me that I hadn't paid. There was very little English spoken and I didn't understand what the problem was, so the receptionist tried to converse with me using a piece of translation software on the reception desk computer. That would have been fine if the software had worked, but she entered Japanese and the output was what I'd call 'Janglish'. Presumably, the same happened when I typed in my English, but the staff were very polite and obviously had more belief in the software than I did. How could I use it to tell them that the output was incomprehensible? Anyway, I eventually got the gist and paid up.

In the meantime, I was looking for a printing facility to print some English maps of Japan which my son had e-mailed me. Across the road was an internet café above a Pachinko parlour. Pachinko parlours are home to the popular Japanese pastime of playing a type of pinball game. Gambling is illegal in Japan, so the player's reward is to keep the balls they have played. These are then exchanged for prizes which, in turn, can be exchanged for cash elsewhere. Rows and rows of zombie-faced punters sat playing and the noise was deafening. I found the internet café as quickly as I could and printed my maps.

Cycling is a popular means of experiencing the Shimanami Kaido. The road is predominantly a car highway but the bridge sections are open to cyclists and pedestrians. The bicycle route is well marked and maintained, and diverges from the expressway on the islands. The ramps leading up to the bridges were built with small inclines with cyclists in mind. At roughly seventy kilometres, the bike route is slightly longer than the expressway, but because there are no steep inclines, it can be comfortably completed in a day. Imabari, the last port on the Shikoku mainland, was obviously geared up for tourists and I was able to buy an English map of the sea-bridge route and head for the first bridge.

By now, it was the end of Golden Week and the towns on Ikuchi Island were virtually closed. I finally found a Japanese B&B or 'minshuku' – not the cheapest type of accommodation, but in this case, the only one. My room was devoid of furniture apart from one small side table, and had a traditional tatami, or rush floor with its sweet, grassy smell. Tatami mats are a fixed size and rooms are built to fit. In Japan, a room is described by the number of mats they can take, for example 'a six-tatami room'. My futon bed was stored in a cupboard – minimalist but perfectly adequate.

Crossing the bridges from one island to another was a thrill. Each bridge was a different type, ranging from cable-stayed to suspension. The Shimanami Kaido is a popular route with locals and bicycle hire is provided at a number of points. There are cycle paths almost all the way, except for across the last bridge, where cyclists must catch the ferry to Onomichi on Honshu.

From Onomichi, I made my way to Kurashiki where my son lived on my first visit to Japan. I'd arranged to stay with one of his friends and as I rode into the city I began to recognise some of the roads. Yukie met me in a coffee bar at the station and later took me out to dinner. In the restaurant, dining parties each had their own private cubicle and as we entered ours, it looked as if we would be sitting on the floor. Thankfully, there was a well under the table to drop your legs into if you so desired – I did. Our meal consisted of sushi, sashimi (raw fish), squid balls, yakitori (kebabs), and a delicious plate of roast onion covered in a carbonara sauce, all washed down with jugs of Kirin beer.

The next morning, Yukie took me to a nearby bookshop where I bought a road atlas for the rest of the Honshu route, the purchase made so much easier with Yukie's help.

Honshu is the largest island in the Japan archipelago and the route I had planned would be along its southern coast. For the next two days, I detoured round peninsulas along the coastline, seeing beautiful scenery and pretty fishing villages, but then the journey began in earnest and I joined the through-traffic to Osaka.

Cycling on the pavement is less stressful but it takes longer to make headway because of the number of traffic lights. I wasn't complaining – the few times I needed to join the trucks and cars because of the absence of a pavement, I couldn't wait for one to appear. Miraculously, I got through Osaka without incident, apart from a mishap when I came too close to an umbrella and my jacket got hooked. A grazed knee but no damage otherwise.

From Osaka, I cycled to Kyoto, formerly the capital of Japan and full of ancient buildings. Because of its historical significance, it was spared attack during WWII and is one of the best preserved cities in the country. I'd toured the main sites with my family on the first visit, so this time I made do with another look at its futuristic train station. Kyoto station opened in 1997, commemorating the city's 1,200th anniversary and is one of Japan's largest buildings. It is 70 metres high, 470 metres from east to west, and has a floor area of 238,000 square metres. Around its edges, the shopping malls are labyrinthine and I nearly gave up trying to find the main hall. Finally, I emerged in the vast cathedral space in the centre. There is so much to see there, that you could wander round for hours.

Trying to stick to Route 1 was like an orienteering test at times. It took me over cycle bridges and through underpasses, sometimes with little or no signage for the poor cyclist. There were occasions when I had to leave Route 1 because I hit a section of toll road. This often meant going through more scenic areas and added to the excitement of hoping I was actually going the right way. When I remembered how long it took me to get out of St Omer in France with an English map, it made me think I must have learned a thing or two since then.

One diversion brought me down the side of Lake Hamana, a large sea lake where I counted five aqueducts traversing the narrow spits of land on the edge of the Pacific Ocean. It was a beautiful sunny day and I could see people across the lake fishing. Life was good.

I stayed at Hamamatsu that night and set out for Shizuoka the next day. I knew this stretch was going to be difficult, because the map showed tunnels and bypasses in two sections of the road. With twenty miles to go, I stopped on a quiet corner to check for the next stretch of tunnels and bypasses. As I perused the map with magnifying glass in hand, a Japanese cyclist of mature years like myself stopped to help. He didn't speak English but he made it clear that I would have no problem getting to Shizuoka on my bike. I thanked him for his help with an “aregato” (thank you), and got going. The trouble was that he continued to cycle alongside me on the road as I pedalled on the pavement. 'Where is he going?' I wondered. The miles wore on and he stuck to me like glue. I couldn't ask why, because of the language problem and I still had twenty miles to go. I kept thinking I'd shaken him off, because I was sometimes able to continue on the pavement when the road traffic had to stop, but no, there he was to my right, as thin as a whippet in his go-faster lycra. I was becoming more than a little irritated when he started pointing out my crossing points and holding his hand up to stop approaching cars. Trying to convey the fact that I didn't need his help and I'd actually cycled all the way from Kyushu made no difference.

Ten miles on and I'd accepted that he was there to stay. When he stopped me from turning right and said “No – old road”, meaning stay on this one, I began to think maybe I should be glad of his company. We eventually came to a small town where he stopped me and said, “Tea time?” Well, at least he knew what a tea-shop was, unlike me, who couldn't read the signs. I was ready for a break so we went into a small café that he obviously frequented.

We sat down and as we waited for our tea, he did something that totally astonished me – he detached his left leg below the knee. Shimizu lived in Shizuoka (as I found out from the proprietor's daughter) and was cycling at least forty miles with only one and a half legs. I would have liked to find out how he had lost the leg, but of course that was impossible. I could only show my amazement and appreciation of his stamina.

We finished our green tea and bean curd fondant, which Shimizu paid for, and set off. Filled with guilt for my uncharitable feelings, I followed as he guided me along the old Route 1 road. This time we were a team.

We rode together through breath-taking mountainous scenery and eventually entered a tunnel close to Shizuoka City. This one was far less arduous than any of the previous ones. The cycling path was wide enough for the two of us to ride side-by-side, and coming out the far end, we headed for the city centre. Shimizu stayed with me until we reached the station and it was with a pang of sorrow that I shook hands with him and said goodbye. He gave me a card with a Japanese telephone number on but I couldn't reciprocate. Nor could I ask him if he had an email address. His card didn't show one, so I guessed not.

Further up the coast I was in full view of Mount Fuji for most of one day. I first saw this mountain from a train when I visited the country three years previously. Travelling with my children, it was just luck that I happened to look up and see the snow-capped peak hanging in the sky above the clouds. It was an impossibly beautiful site and I swear I heard angels sing. This time the same overwhelming feeling struck me – only I went weak at the knees as well.

The journey from Numazu was to take me over a mountainous area across the neck of a peninsula, before returning to the coast. The road up the mountain was steep and it forked towards either the Atami Pass or the town of Atami – which I knew would take me through a tunnel. However, this time I chose the tunnel. My recent experience had been favourable and going through the mountain was bound to be infinitely less steep than going over it.

I stopped beside the road for lunch, and while I was enjoying the view and speculating as to whether I was looking at the steeper route, it occurred to me that I ought to be able to see Mt Fuji – then I raised my sights higher to the right and picked out its snow-capped peak hanging there like an iced cake among the clouds – magical.

This time, the tunnel wasn't too difficult, but it was long – 1250m. The pavement at the side was only a metre wide and walking Sofi through took fifteen minutes. Every so often, mud seeping through the sides made the path slippery and it required extra concentration in certain places. I exited after the ordeal with white knuckles, only to find there was another tunnel in front of me, (...so much for there always being a light at the end of the tunnel)! Happily, the second one was much shorter. The road down into Atami was steep and winding, forcing me to stop halfway to cool my brakes.

At the bottom of the hill, I could see the coast again and the road undulated as it crept along the hillside. Riding became more difficult as the paths and hard shoulder disappeared and the traffic increased. There were short tunnels on the way and eventually the road veered downhill to sea level.

As I sped along, a young, athletic, Japanese cyclist flew past and shouted 'konichiwa' (hello). I returned his greeting and a couple of miles on, he flagged me down to chat. His English was excellent and we talked about the ride over the mountain. I commented that I hadn't particularly enjoyed the last part of the journey and it was probably not going to improve for a while, because there would shortly be a tricky bypass to negotiate. "No – it's very easy," he said and told me to follow him. We rode off and he led me through a maze of backstreets until we arrived at the old Route 1. I counted myself very lucky to have met him.

There was no standing under bridges, no scratching my head and no wondering how to get round.

The next day should have been a straightforward thirty-mile ride to my son's flat in the north west of Tokyo, but it didn't quite turn out that way.

Matthew was working and wouldn't be home until 4.30pm, so I took my time setting off and ambled along the pavements of the '129'. There was an alternative, quieter route to the west but it looked hillier, so I decided to stay on the 129 for as long as I could. After a few miles and a few flyovers, the road was becoming less and less attractive and I branched off it, to take the other route. This was fine for a while, until the road signs began to disappear and I found myself completely lost. Up to now, I'd been feeling quite confident about getting to Tokyo, but crossing a major city turned out to be no easy task. I'd cycled for five miles when I found myself back on the 129, just a mile further north from where I'd started. Things were not going well. The weather then took a serious turn for the worse and I found myself going round in circles in pouring rain. In the heart of the city, the road I needed evaded me at every attempt. My only option was to make a long detour east, where I could see an easier way to join the road I wanted heading northwest. Trying to access it through the main arteries just wasn't working and I hoped that once on it, it should be well signed with road numbers.

By now it was 4.30 and I was in full waterproofs, struggling to read a disintegrating map with reading glasses and a magnifying glass. I was soaked when I found a phone box to tell my son where I was. He gave me some instructions and waited for my next call.

Luckily, my plan worked and I found myself travelling in the right direction, but it was 8.30 by now and dark. I'd cycled through some quiet rural areas, worried for much of the time that I would find myself heading into the hills behind Tokyo.

I made the last call to tell my son I was at the nearby station. He came to meet me on his bicycle and, after much hugging, we cycled to his apartment. It had been a gruelling day finding my way across Tokyo but it was all worth it and nice to know I would be with a loved one for a rather special birthday – my 60th.

My time in Tokyo was mainly spent relaxing, with visits to local restaurants with my son and his friends. Sofi was once again boxed and it was collected by courier and taken to the airport. Matthew and I took the train there for an emotional goodbye.

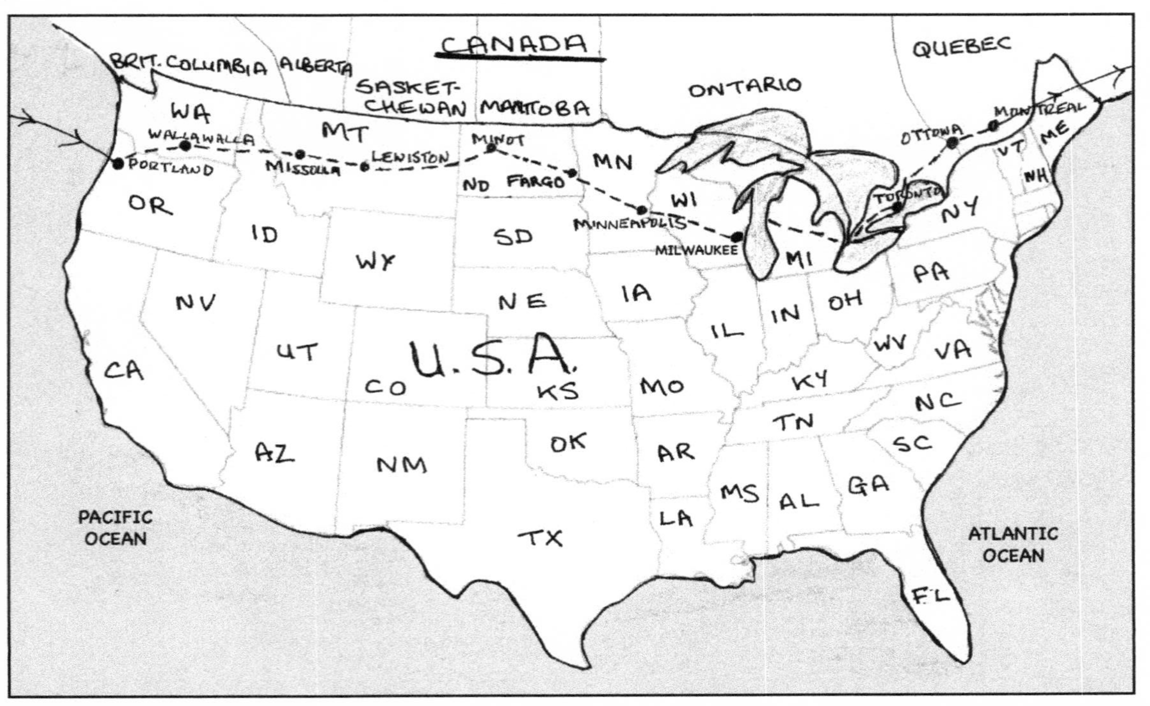
CANADA
BRIT. COLUMBIA
ALBERTA
SASKET-
CHEWAN
MANITOBA
ONTARIO
QUEBEC
WA
WALLAWALLA
PORTLAND
MT
MISSOULA
LEWISTON
MINOT
ND
FARGO
MN
MINNEAPOLIS
WI
MILWAUKEE
MI
TORONTO
OTTOWA
MONTREAL
VT
ME
NH
NY
OR
ID
WY
SD
PA
NV
NE
IA
IN
OH
U.S.A.
IL
WV
VA
CA
UT
CO
KS
MO
KY
NC
TN
AZ
NM
OK
AR
SC
MS
AL
GA
LA
TX
FL
PACIFIC
OCEAN
ATLANTIC
OCEAN

North America

"Hello Bruv"

I left Tokyo on a Sunday afternoon and because of the time difference, arrived in Portland on the same morning – quite nifty, this time travelling.

The passport officials were not best pleased that I didn't have an onward flight booked but they begrudgingly let me through. When I questioned the requirement of an onward flight, because having one wouldn't necessarily stop me staying in the country, one of the officers barked at me "You screwed up!" I thought it best not to argue.

Feeling suitably told off, I made my way to the outsize luggage reclaim area, only to find that all my packing and duct-taping handiwork on the bike box had been sliced through and it was now held together with sellotape. Thank goodness for the hotel shuttle service and a very helpful driver.

The maps I used to cross the United States are produced by the Adventure Cycling Association (ACA), a non-profit organisation established in 1973, which has created one of the largest route networks in the world, covering almost 48,000 miles of North American roads. My eldest brother lives in Milwaukee, Wisconsin and had posted the first one I needed to the airport hotel. This would take me to Missoula in Montana, where the ACA has its headquarters and where I could buy more maps.

My plan was to follow the ACA Lewis and Clarke route east until it met the Northern Tier route at Williston in North Dakota. Captain Meriwether Lewis and Second Lieutenant William Clark, after whom the route was named, were two

U.S. Army volunteers who led an expedition in 1804 to cross the previously-unexplored western part of the country. From Williston, I would continue to Minneapolis and then on to Milwaukee to visit my brother. The rest of the route was, as yet, unplanned.

For most of the time in Oregon, the weather was dreadful and I was cycling in waterproof coat and trousers. The scenery however, was possibly the most beautiful I'd ever seen. Mountains and rivers so vast that my own Lake District in England seemed like a tiny miniature version. Even the mist and rain didn't hide the stunning splendour of the magnificent vistas, and the hoarse bark of the freight train as it travelled along the banks of the River Columbia never failed to raise a tingle in my spine – I hadn't realised its evocative sound was still in use, and not just a relic of black and white Western films. Romantic sounding towns lay in front of me – Cascade Locks, Hood River, Pelican Rapids; would I ever get used to these names.

A section of the Interstate Highway was being upgraded and when I was diverted onto the main road, my map instructions made no sense at all. Amazingly, I got through, but not without expecting to be squashed to a paste as the trucks thundered past spraying me with water. Away from the highway, things were much more tranquil, too tranquil at times and it was odd to be on good roads with so little traffic, just the occasional car – silent enough to make me feel quite isolated.

The road rose steeply above the river and I was back to pushing. It was a good road, 'paved all the way to Mosier' I was told by some passing cyclists, and it was. I was passing through the Tom McCall Preserve, an area named after Oregon's late governor Thomas Lawson McCall, in memory of his commitment to conservation in Oregon. Again, there were few cars and the road afforded some magnificent views across the river. From Troutdale to The Dalles, I followed a cycle path overlooking the Columbia River Highway and taking me through the Columbia

River Gorge to cross the Cascade Mountains. This was the first modern highway constructed in the Pacific Northwest and also the first scenic highway ever built in the United States. No wonder the views were so spectacular.

I passed The Dalles and carried on to Biggs Junction, a service area on the south side of the river, with a number of motels, eateries and fuel stations. Below me, the Sam Hill Memorial Bridge spanned the Columbia River, which I would cross in the morning into Washington State. On the far side, I could see a very steep hill looking at me.

The forecast for the next day was poor and I left around eleven to take it slowly to a campsite forty-one miles away. The last thing I wanted to do was get there early, only to sit in my tent in the wind and the dark. Summiting the hill a few miles from the bridge, I could see a stone structure in the distance that puzzled me. Was it a fort? A castle? This, I couldn't miss, and making a short detour, came across a WWI memorial replica of Stonehenge. The public can no longer walk among the stones in England but here I could. Maryhill Stonehenge was built in 1924 and may not be as old as the original, but I found my visit a peaceful and moving experience. That such a huge structure had been built for only 17 men was very impressive. In England, I'd seen much smaller monuments for many more heroes, but then again, this was America.

Luck was obviously on my side, as the sun came out and it was dry all day. A strong tail wind bounced me along like a ping-pong ball for the next eighty-five miles, and if I stopped for any reason, I was nearly blown over from behind. I flew like the wind along the Columbia riverside road and, as it was mostly downhill, I reached a speed of thirty-nine miles per hour at one point, and had to slow myself down (I'm not that brave when it comes to speed). How sorry I felt for the two Swedish cyclists I met coming the opposite way. They'd been forced to rest for half an hour to recover from the exhaustion of battling against the wind and talked of possibly cycling through the night when the gusts should be less strong. For me, the ride beside the Columbia River was thrilling. The air was clear and the view across the hydroelectric dams was stunning. I'd passed two campsites by 5pm and with the wind still driving me on, pressed on to cross the border back into Oregon at Umatilla, where I found a reasonably priced motel.

The following morning, I was heading once again into Washington State to the town of Walla Walla, but a mile out of Umatilla I could feel my back wheel bumping along. On examination, the back tyre had a hole in it as big as my thumb. I rolled back down the hill to town and heard a loud bang as the tube exploded.

So – what to do now? There was no bike shop marked on the ACA map in Umatilla and the next one on my route was at Walla Walla. I asked at a service station if any of the truck drivers were going that way but the answer was no. It looked like I'd be staying another night in the town while I caught a bus to Walla Walla to get a new tyre. I headed back to the motel to enquire. "Sorry – no buses at this town", I was told, "but there's a bike shop in Hermiston six miles away". After some negotiation, a young girl from the motel agreed to drive me with bike and bags to the bike shop for twenty dollars. That was fine by me. Would it have been worth carrying a spare tyre all this way? – I don't think so.

The mechanics at Scott's Bike shop were very helpful and regaled me with their tales about black bears. A young one had once climbed into the back of their truck. "It's not the bears you have to worry about – it's the cats!" they told me with a grin. They changed the tyre, equipped me with a spare tube and a map to get out of town, and I left around noon.

I was now travelling in a northerly direction and even though the wind wasn't so co-operative, I still managed the sixty-five miles to Walla Walla by late evening. By now I was beyond hungry and went to a Chinese Restaurant where I ate a huge plate of chicken chop suey. The last ten miles had been a struggle and I slept like a baby.

Rain fell steadily for the next two days and the hills became much steeper. I finally reached the last summit and saw signs warning truck drivers to check their brakes - always a good clue for the cyclist that a long downhill cruise will follow. Over the top, my efforts were rewarded with an exhilarating, effortless ride towards Clarkston. It went on and on for twelve miles - you could hardly call it cycling really, it was such a breeze.

At the bottom of the hill, the weather was so much improved that I camped for the first time since Slovenia, in the Chief Timothy Park campsite. The park, named after one of the Nez Perce tribal chiefs, covers a small island in Snake River and is surrounded by mountains – an idyllic location. There was only one other camper in the expansive tent area and he was in the distance. That enabled me to brush up my long lost tent-pitching skills without an audience. It was a beautiful evening and squirrels and wild albino rabbits ran around as I ate sandwiches made with the squashed remains of my larder. It was hard to believe how easy life had become, especially now that everyone spoke English.

Again the weather was variable as I headed for Winchester. There was lots of pushing uphill and then – oh no! – not another flat! I pulled into a driveway on the quiet road, unloaded the bike and turned it on its head. As I ran my fingers around the inside of the tyre I found not one but multiple thorns sticking through. On closer examination of the outside, the tyre was like a pincushion and I rooted out my tweezers to clear them. 'Thorns' was too good a name for these spikes. These were goathead seeds which are like tiny sharp-headed sputniks. No doubt about it, if the back one was damaged, so was the front. I inspected the front tyre and as I pulled out a large prickle, the tube hissed and the air escaped. It must have happened when I was pushing up the side of the road on a soft shoulder. By the time I'd plucked all the spikes out, changed the tubes and cycled to Winchester, it was 9.30pm and dark. I checked in at the first place I could find.

The bad weather continued for the next few days and the pressure was on because motels were becoming scarce. Trussed up again in my waterproofs, I was now in Idaho and riding beside the raging Clearwater River, with steep banks on my right and no safety barriers. The heavy rain meant visibility was bad and it took serious concentration to stay on the road. I just hoped there wouldn't be too many hills to slow me down. Also battling with the rain were cyclists Clyde and Joelle, and we chatted as we met intermittently throughout the course of the day. The bad news was that Joelle had rung ahead to the Lochsa Lodge, where we were hoping to stay, and it was full. A large party of water sports enthusiasts had made a block booking and our only hope was that they might cancel because of the bad weather – they didn't. There were, however, two campsites in the grounds and the owner of the Lodge allowed us to camp for free, as long as we ate in the restaurant. We had little choice, and luckily, the rain abated long enough for us to pitch our tents. After a welcome hot meal, I spent the evening in the lounge chatting to Clyde and Joelle, and Todd, Tim and Marty, more cyclists who had arrived ahead of us. Todd, a big man with a big smile, was sure all six of us must come from the "Land of Stoopid!" to be out in such weather. It was congenial company and we had a very pleasant evening in spite of the water-sports revellers keeping me awake until 11.30. I thought I'd got away quite lightly at that.

Saturday dawned on a beautiful day and a hefty breakfast of eggs, bacon and pancakes set me up to tackle the 1500 ft Lolo Pass. Nothing seems so bad when the sun is shining and I'd reached the top by 2pm. At the crest of the hill, I left Idaho and entered Montana and a new time zone. With another enjoyable sail down the pass to the town of Lolo, and a further thirteen-mile ride, I reached Missoula, the headquarters of the Adventure Cycling Association.

The next morning I was in the ACA office perusing maps when I looked up to see the smiling face of Todd through the window. He and his friends were following another cross-country route, the TransAmerican, and Tim and Marty soon rolled up. These guys were great company and I was so glad to see them. The four of us spent that night in Hutchins Hostel and dined at a nearby Thai restaurant. The next day, I said goodbye once again and set off, while the boys returned to the ACA headquarters to look at maps.

In two days I'd reached Darby and as I came out of the local supermarket, who should appear but Marty. The group had caught up with me and gained another team member, Peggy. I was so pleased to see them all and it wasn't long before I was invited to cycle with them to Sula and tackle the Chief Joseph Pass the next day.

Thirty-three miles later, when we arrived at the campsite in Sula, a downpour started and we were relieved to get out of the rain. Todd, Peggy and I took advantage of the hot-tub hut, where we could soak in the heat with a glass of wine and look out the windows at the rain. Our little group, now five, gathered in the men's cabin for a meal. It was such a pleasure to find myself in convivial company after spending so long travelling on my own.

On the Chief Joseph Pass, we were soon above the snow-line with large flakes obliterating the view and everything overlain with white. Thick piles of snow weighed down the fir trees and a quiet stillness filled the air. The others struggled to pedal all the way up the pass whereas I, as usual, dismounted and pushed. "Why don't you get off and walk?", I said to Tim, who wasn't making much more progress than me. "If I wanted to walk, I wouldn't have brought my bike!", came back the cynical response. At the visitor centre at the summit we were rewarded with free hot coffee, supplied by the forest rangers to warm our bones.

We left our next stop, Wisdom, on a beautiful day, with every view a postcard shot. The rivers were still swollen with rain, and water was standing in the lowest levels. There was some discussion about stopping at Jackson, our earlier target, but we'd made good progress and agreed to press on to a campsite close to a ghost town in Bannack State Park.

Bannack ghost town is the site of a major gold discovery in the mid-19th century. The town is fairly unusual in that it is in the process of preservation, whereas others in the west have been left to deteriorate. Visitors can wander along the wooden sidewalks of the main street and enter houses which would have been full of life during the gold rush. The original wallpaper can still be seen in many buildings, and the hotel even has a renovated stove in its kitchen. The school's old desks have survived, and it's easy to imagine a time when the room would be full of children. We spent some time there in the morning before a late start heading for Twin Bridges, where my friends and I would part, as I continued on the Lewis and Clarke Trail east, and they followed the TransAmerican cycle route south.

All was going well until one of my gear cables snapped at a place called Beaver Rock. Between us, we ended up with a temporary repair, but I needed to go back thirteen miles to a bike shop in Dillon. This meant an early goodbye to the group. We had made such a good team, and under different circumstances I would have been only too pleased to stay on the TransAm with them. This wasn't to be. I was sad to leave them but I was heading east to visit my brother.

In a rather sombre mood, I limped back to Dillon and without much hope, because it was a Sunday, rang the bike shop. My luck had changed and Joe the owner was there and happy to help. Working on a bike that had travelled so far was a treat for him. "Most of the ones I fix have only been to the shops and back," he said. He gave Sofi a thorough service and replaced the broken cable, the cassette, chain and front tyre. For anyone cycling through Dillon, you'd do well to give him a ring if your bike needs attention.

The next day, Sofi was flying, and with a strong tailwind, I cycled the thirteen miles back to Beaver Rock in no time at all. The tailwind carried on throughout the afternoon and another fifty miles on, I was passing through a deep gorge lined with impressive rock exposures interspersed with natural pine forests. By evening I'd arrived at the Lewis and Clarke State Park campsite, set in a valley surrounded by hills, and with the most amazing birdlife on show – bright orange Baltimore oriels and deep blue pinyon jays.

In the morning, an 'elderly' couple (like myself I suppose) came to collect the campsite fee and told me that they were 'Snowbirds'. They had sold their house to buy an R.V. and now followed the sun, working part of the time as campsite wardens. It sounded like a great life.

The scenery became flatter as I carried on through Montana, across vast plains which deceived the eye. At one point I could see nothing in front of me, only blue sky, and what looked like deep gullies on either side. There was no sign of the town I was looking for, until the road took a surprising dip and descended into the flood plain of the Missouri river. There, in front of me and beside the river, was the pretty little town of Fort Benton. I camped there overnight and climbed back up to the plains the next day. Once again, the town disappeared behind me like an American Brigadoon – quite magical.

The road from Wolf Point took me through the Fort Peck Indian reservation and onto the junction with the Northern Tier route. I was soon to leave the Lewis and Clarke Trail and head east through North Dakota.

Riding to Williston, there was another strong easterly wind behind me and I met cyclist Don coming the other way. At the same time, another cyclist, Chris, rode up behind me. We all stopped to chat and Chris and I felt so sorry for Don who could hardly ride against the headwind. Chris was on a mission to meet a deadline and sped off, leaving us to talk. What a gent Don was: "What are you?" he said, "about thirty-nine?" – such a charmer. "Me?" I said, looking round to see if someone else had appeared, "what? – around the waist?" We laughed, and exchanged stories about our trips. I do hope he managed to continue and that the wind eventually died down for him.

The notes on the ACA map addenda warned of a lack of accommodation in Williston, Dakota due to the amount of new oil activity in the area. Soon drilling machines and 'nodding donkey' pumps dotted the scenery for miles around. Dusty pickups were everywhere. In Stanley, the motels were full and I was told the city park was too. Local residents were wary of the influx of labour and warned me off camping in the park. I eventually found a room in the Bull Moose Inn, a guest house with walls covered in animal trophies, and a very large gun safe taking pride of place in the living room. In the next town, the situation was the same. Campsites and motels full and the only room I could find was an expensive one in a Holiday Inn. Hopefully, things would improve as I left the oil exploration area.

A few miles out of Minot, a young man rode up behind me on his bike. This was another Joe, the leader of a supported ACA group riding from coast-to-coast. He was in charge of a party of eight cyclists of varying ages on a variety of cycles, from a folding Bike Friday to recumbents. The Bike Friday was ridden by Gloria, a seventy-year-old lady, who pulled a trailer and ate copious amounts of ice cream. The men told me later that they struggled to keep up with her. Although I didn't cycle with the group, I spent four nights camping with them in city parks and campsites. The first was at Rugby, famous for being the geographical centre of North America.

On the way to Hope, I realised it was exactly twelve months since I'd left home. Now in the United States, it was hard to take in; did I really cycle all that way? I stopped in Cooperstown, looking for a bottle of something alcoholic to celebrate with the other cyclists, but this was North Dakota on a Sunday and there was no chance. It would have been a completely dry celebration if one of Joe's group hadn't offered me a can of beer he'd managed to buy from a local.

As I reached the end of North Dakota, the land was busy growing crops and the grass was long and lush from all the rain. Big bales of hay stood in the fields and grasshoppers and dragonflies scattered from the road as my wheels approached. In one field, I came across a herd of bison – awesome creatures at close quarters – but not too close.

The Norther Tier route splits at Fargo, and on leaving the city, I took the shorter southern alternative via Dalbo, while Joe's group continued in the Grand Rapids direction, east.

Minnesota claims to be 'The State of 10,000 Lakes' and it would seem so. Lakes of every size and shape surrounded the roads, threatening to overflow in this very wet year. As instructed on my ACA map, when I reached the town of Bowlus, I checked in at Jordie's Café, to camp in the city park opposite. There I met Jordie, the owner. What a delightful lady, so friendly and warm and totally thrilled to hear my story – so much so, that she promised me a free breakfast in the morning. Feeling quite uplifted, I wheeled across to the park to pitch my tent. As I was unpacking, two young men rolled up on bicycles – I wasn't quite sure what Jan was riding, but it turned out he'd modified it for the local parade. The frame was wrapped in brown fur and the handlebars sported real cow horns. Jan and his wife Jenny are Warm Showers hosts and are keen to invite cyclists to their home to hear their stories. They already had guests, but I was welcome to camp in their garden and use the bathroom. After three hot days cycling without a shower, I gladly accepted and spent a lovely evening with Jan and Jenny and their guests, over barbecued sausages and beer. The next morning we went to Jordie's for breakfast, and true to her word, mine was on the house.

My next stop was at Minneapolis to meet Beth. She'd read my journal and given me helpful advice on crossing America. Now she was going to give me some maps of bike trails across Wisconsin, which would take me to my brother in Milwaukee. Beth and her partner Rebecca treated me to a delicious home-cooked meal, the first for a long time. When I left, Beth cycled part of the way with me, then I continued on to cross the mighty Mississippi into Wisconsin.

My hosts had recommended a visit to 'The Rock in the House' in Fountain City. There was no one around when I arrived and the front door was open. It was difficult not to feel like an intruder as I read the hand-written notes telling visitors to pay their dollar to the tin and enter the house. A few dim lights illuminated the interior, and in the background, you could hear a radio playing old-style music. The house felt as if it had been frozen in time. On the walls, black and white photographs recorded the past, and news cuttings on pin boards described the event that had made the house an attraction. It wasn't until I opened the back door and saw the fifty-five-ton rock that I could see the devastation. In 1995, the megalith had rolled down the hill behind and landed in the bedroom, rendering the house uninhabitable. Nothing had been touched since the event and I felt distinctly uncomfortable being there on my own – as if I was invading someone's privacy. I didn't linger.

I camped that night in the Merrick State Park and got eaten alive by mosquitoes, both in and out of my tent. It rained all night and continued until 10am when I ventured out. There was no chance of drying my tent so I packed it up wet and heavy and set off to find my first bike path, the Great River State Trail. Friday took me onto the Elroy/Sparta trail, the first trail in the State to be converted from a disused railway line. Conditions were great for cycling but this stretch involved passing through three tunnels, one of which was nearly a mile long. The first was the longest one, and apart from the daylight permeating for the first few yards, it was totally unlit. As the entrance shrank behind me, I was shrouded in the blackest of black. My head torch cast a very thin light as I scanned from side to side to avoid walking into the walls or the water-filled gutters. In the damp and the cold it seemed to go on forever, and it was easy to let your imagination run wild and expect a firm hand to suddenly plant itself on your shoulder. What a relief it was to see that tiny dot of light growing larger as I reached the end.

I crossed Madison to ride the Glacial Drumlin Trail and joined the New Berlin bike path which would take me to the Oak Leaf Trail.

As I entered the outskirts of Milwaukee, I rang my brother who told me to look out for yellow balloons. Really…? But true enough, along the trail I spotted happy smiley helium balloons fastened to fences and posts, welcoming me to the city. I collected each one, tying them to the back of my bike, until I reached my brother's house where he and his wife were waiting to meet me. I'd travelled ninety percent of the way across the State on bike trails and paths. Wisconsin really does deserve its reputation as one of the most bike-friendly states in America.

I spent a week with my family, and at the end of my visit, Terry cycled with me for the first mile out of town. I was once again on the Oak Leaf Trail, but this time heading north to Manitowoc to take a ferry across Lake Michigan.

The road from Sheboygan hugged the lake for much of the way and was lined with prestigious properties, many with lake frontage. I'd done sixty-six miles by the time I reached the ferry port and my legs were complaining. Seven days out of the saddle were beginning to tell. Happily, the only daytime ferry crossing was at 1.55pm the next day. That meant a day's rest for the old quads.

Before long I was approaching Canada and there were over 3,000 miles behind me in the USA. Crossing the States had always seemed like the biggest hurdle in so many ways, but in the end it was the easiest, if not the shortest. The ACA maps had been a great help, directing me away from major roads and showing me where to stay at night.

As the days wore on, for some reason I began to feel I wasn't cycling very well. One morning I was almost tempted to stop at 'Woodyzzz Motel' after only thirty miles, but as it was early, I pressed on. A mile or so down the road, another cyclist pulled up behind me and we stopped to chat. Jack was following the same route and we were happy to cycle together. He was keen to hear about my journey, and I was more than interested in his travel stories, especially about Pakistan and India. What had been arduous cycling became so much easier as we exchanged our tales of adventure. I realised that my fatigue had happened because I was getting used to having company again, and missed it when it wasn't there.

We checked in at the next campsite, and I discovered that Joe's ACA group were just one day ahead of me now and had stayed there the previous night. When I left them at Fargo, they were heading north while I turned south in the direction of Milwaukee. What a coincidence that I should be only one day behind as we crossed routes again along the Lake Erie Connector.

Jack and I reached the town of St Clair after sixty-three miles more and I didn't have another twelve left in me to get to the next campsite. Jack carried on and I opted for a hotel. Murphy's Hotel was very comfortable but expensive, and I waited until the checkout time of noon, to get as much value out of it as I could. I took my time over a breakfast of bagels and fresh fruit, chatted to my son on Skype and updated my journal. I was well rested but I would pay the price of leaving so late by the end of the day.

The ferry linking North America with Canada crosses the St Clair River in Marine City. The guards there were much more friendly than the ones in Portland and they waved me through with a permit until the end of October.

Canada

Chocolate Covered Bacon

The difference after crossing into Canada wasn't immediately any greater than when passing into a new state in America. The houses beside the azure blue St Clair River seemed very prestigious, but then they were probably the more expensive ones, having river frontage.

I battled on against the wind, aiming for a campsite in Morpeth, but by the time I got there, the light was failing and I couldn't find the road I was looking for. It got progressively darker as I searched, until I knew I would have to find a spot, anywhere, to make camp. I came across a church with a neatly mown cemetery and sneaked in, wedging myself behind a large fir tree. As soon as the grass beneath me was disturbed, thousands of mosquitoes rose from it. I've never pitched my tent so fast. The next morning, covered in lumps and bumps, I made my getaway and left not a mark behind.

The nearest café was five miles away and when I stopped for breakfast, who should appear but John, one of Joe's ACA group, shortly followed by Joe himself. Amazing that our paths should diverge for so many miles and yet here we were at the same time, in the same place. It was a great reunion and they invited me to camp with them at Port Burwell.

When I rolled into the campsite, it was such a pleasure to see all the familiar faces and I readily agreed to join them for campsite dinner. I pitched my tent and headed towards the showers. On the way, Linda from one of the static camper vehicles beckoned and loaded me up with huge bowls of chopped melon to share with the group. Everyone was delighted when I returned with my arms full of fruit, and even more pleased when Linda brought a large pot of coffee to us after the meal. In the morning, the group had moved on by the time I woke up.

Niagara Falls weren't immediately that easy to find because of a traffic diversion, but the directions of a helpful young man brought me to the wondrous sight. I was so glad to see it from the Canadian side, as the view from the opposite bank of the river is not as impressive.

I'd rung ahead to book a couple of nights in a backpackers hostel on the far side of the tourist area. This part of the town is not such a pretty sight. Its tawdry commercialisation is typical of the worst kind of seaside attractions. The hostel was run by a crabby old man, who in spite of telling me over the phone that the bike would be "no trouble", in fact meant that it would be no trouble to him, because I would have to leave it outside. From me, it was a case of "Thank you and goodbye", and I left, hearing him saying, "You'll have difficulty finding a place that isn't full". Well, that was patently untrue, because I passed a number of motels with vacancies and chose a very reasonable one run by a Serbian family. The room in the Riverview Motel was spotless and the owners more than happy to hear about my visit to their country last year.

Nearby Queen Street in the residential part of the city was a complete contrast to the tourist area. Attractive shops and restaurants lined the thoroughfare and it was difficult to imagine that the mayhem of the funfair and haunted houses was only a mile away.

There was one shop that really intrigued me, advertising above the doorway – 'Chocolate Covered Bacon'. In the true spirit of adventure, I had to try it and can say that chocolate-covered bacon is VERY good.

Canada is a melting pot of nationalities and I saw and heard people of all races in a very short space of time. The British influence is alive and well however, and I was seeing so many things that reminded me of home, such as fish and chip shops, Sotheby's signs and so many British place names – Northumberland, Durham and even a town called Bronte.

In Toronto, my Warm Shower host David looked after me admirably. I arrived wet and bedraggled and, after hosing down my filthy bike and bags, I was soon under a hot shower and then presented with a home-cooked pasta meal, and a couple of glasses of red wine. I said goodbye to David the next morning and re-joined the Waterfront cycle route to take me out of the city.

In the lovely town of Bowmanville, I spotted a shop selling British goods and finally found some Marmite. I'd been looking for it since Portland without success (you have to be English to understand the Marmite thing). In Port Hope, I tried Canadian fish and chips and they were mouth-watering, very like the ones in England. I felt like a new woman as I pedalled off after my meal.

Wednesday was the day my odometer tripped the magic number – 10,000 miles. It was hard to believe that I'd cycled almost 3,000 miles in America so easily. The first 5,000 miles of my journey had seemed so difficult at times and it brought home to me how much slower my progress had been in other parts of the world.

Mary-Lynne in Kingston had read my journal, and realising that I would be virtually passing her door on the outskirts of the city, invited me to stay. What a memorable visit that was. I had dinner with the family, followed by a city tour. Kingston has an interesting history and is called the 'limestone city' for its many impressive buildings constructed in the stone of that name – churches and university halls, the city hall and cathedral, as well as many more military buildings and private houses. As darkness descended, Mary-Lynne's husband, Richard, drove us round to Fort Henry, hoping to catch the end of the Sunset Ceremony where cannons are fired. The fort dates back to 1812. It is no longer a defensive structure and performs re-enactments of historical military displays for the public. We expected to only watch from the outside but when the attendant was told I was English, we were ushered in and saw the end of the performance for free. It was a delight for me, to hear British anthems played by the band, but the highlight was yet to come. At the end of the ceremony, we looked up to see a piper stood on the ramparts, playing against the night sky under a spotlight. The atmosphere was electric.

I left Kingston in the morning and took off north in the direction of Ottawa to visit Rachelle, an old friend of my daughter. Rachelle was married to Flavio, and when we said goodbye in England three years earlier none of us expected I would be visiting them in their home country.

On Sunday, we walked into the centre of the city to see the sights and were treated to all the fun of a Gay Pride parade. In the streets, food vendors were busy serving the crowds. "You've got to try Beavertails", said Rachelle. "Beavertails…?" I asked, "What happens to the rest of the beaver?" "They re-grow their tails" she said mischievously, without cracking a smile. At this point in my journey, anything was possible. They turned out to be a tasty deep-fried dough base with the topping of your choice. Mine was bananas and chocolate.

One evening, Rachelle, Flavio and I crossed the river to Gatineau Park over the Quebec border to walk around Pink Lake, which isn't pink but green because of the algal life it supports. Its name comes from a family of Irish settlers who originally owned the land.

Saturday came and Rachelle and Flavio cycled with me into town where we hugged and hugged some more and said our goodbyes.

I took the road leading out of Ontario and into Quebec. I was now heading for Montreal to stay with yet another of my journal readers, who had offered me accommodation before my flight home on Thursday. I had hoped to make it in two days, but the weather deteriorated and the nights were drawing in. When the skies darkened and threatened rain, I made it a short day and stopped off at Montebello.

Another day I clocked up fifty-eight miles getting to Vaudreuil-sur-Lac via the ferry across the Ottawa River from Oka to Hudson. On the approach to Oka, there were five miles of unsurfaced road through an Indian reservation. My teeth rattled as I bounced along, passing a line of kiosks selling 'native cigarettes'. The economy of the reservation obviously didn't support road repair.

In the previous year, after I landed in India, Roger in Montreal wrote to me on my journal, to tell me he had enjoyed reading about my travels and was thinking about touring Italy. He wished me well and I never forgot his closing words, – "for God's sake, be careful", it seemed such a heartfelt comment. Neither of us knew at the time that I would end up in his city, but when it became clear I would be flying home from there, he invited me to stay.

I arrived at his door late in the morning, and was soon seated with most of the family at his daughter's house, enjoying lunch and being made to feel most welcome. Over the next two days I was taken sightseeing round the city and fed delicious home cooked meals by his wife Joanne. On the afternoon of my departure, I was taken to meet Rosemary, a Scottish friend of Roger and Joanne. She welcomed us and fed us tea and biscuits, but not just ordinary biscuits – these were McVitie's chocolate digestives, all the way from England – bliss! On my last day, Roger and his wife drove me to the airport. Roger's parting words – "and for God's sake, be careful".

England

It's good to be 'ome

It was a rainy afternoon when I arrived in Manchester to be met by my friend Gill, with whom I would be staying for two nights. This gave me time to recover from the flight and the jetlag, and time for us to catch up. It was great to be in England but in many ways I was sorry the adventure was ending. Two nights and then just over a day's ride and I would be home in Ulverston.

A full English breakfast was a great start to the day, as I prepared to cycle north. I set off along a short stretch of road, towards a narrow cycle track behind the local pub and waved as Gill passed me in her car. She was taking my panniers to the far end of the track to make things easy for me. Along the side of a reservoir I stopped to capture a photograph of a completely perfect rainbow from one side of the water to the other. An old chap was walking towards me. "You don't get much better than that", he said, as he passed. It was good to be 'ome.

"You do realise you were on the wrong side of the road don't you?" Gill said as she got out of her car. Oo-err!! No, I hadn't! Good job I didn't meet an oncoming car – could've been wiped out on the last leg.

We said our goodbyes, and paying much more attention, I set off up Greenarms Road, heading north.

As I cycled through the village of Belton, church bells were ringing and two old dears dressed for service in their Sunday best, smiled and said "Hello." Past the terraces of stone houses and church steeples I went, in the direction of Preston. As I got close to Preston, the heavens opened, and before long I was like a drowned rat. The weather improved on the other side of the town and I sat on a village bench to eat the sandwiches prepared for me by Gill. I was now on familiar territory and for the first time in fourteen months, I didn't need a map. Through the historic university town of Lancaster I rode and it was still only 3pm when I reached Carnforth, famous for its station appearing in the classic black and white film, Brief Encounter. I'd been asked to do a radio interview at 8.45am the next morning and it had to be on a land line. That meant that I couldn't leave my lodgings until 9am at the earliest. There was also a TV crew expecting me to arrive in Ulverston at 1pm, so wherever I stayed that night, it had to be within four hours of Ulverston.

I ended up in the village of Beetham, in a B&B close to the local pub, where I dined that night on a splendid meal of belly pork with homemade apple and raisin sauce.

The next morning was fine when I awoke, but the rain started again and I had to don full waterproofs. I'm convinced that English rain is different rain from anywhere else in the world. It's as if the weather gods tune the spray level to somewhere between drizzle and heavy rain and then forget to turn it off. It just goes on and on at a consistent rate.

The water was pooling in my shoes by the time I approached Ulverston. It was only 11.45am, so I rang my daughter and detoured to the tiny chip shop in Greenodd village to meet her. She arrived in a van with a towel, a flask of hot coffee and an abundance of massive hugs. I had my first English fish and chips for a long time. With only four miles to go in the rain, there was no point in trying to dry off, so I sat steaming in the back of the van eating my feast.

On the dot of 1pm, I cycled up to Ulverston's Coronation Hall, where a crowd of family and friends were waiting to cheer my arrival. The Lord Mayor presented me with flowers and gave a speech. In amongst the bustle, I thought I heard the words, 'intrepid cyclist' but it might have been 'dripping cyclist'.

It had been an incredible journey, and I don't know how I would have managed without the help I received along the way from perfect strangers. I am so thankful to them. The main lesson I learned, is that the world is not as dangerous a place as people think, so long as you have your wits about you and don't take uncalculated risks.

Thanks for sticking with me everyone – IT'S BEEN TRULY AMAZING!

Marty, Peggy, Tim and Todd
at the Chief Joseph Pass Visitor Centre

Son Matthew in Tokyo

Rugby, North Dakota. The geographical
centre of North America

Niagara Falls

A rainy day return to Ulverston

Acknowledgements

My thanks go to my daughter Vanessa for her complete faith in my ability and for holding the fort while I was away. Without her help and encouragement this journey might never have happened. Thanks to my son Matthew for helping me find my way across Japan and for looking after me in Tokyo. Thanks to my brother Mike for his PR work and for arranging the fantastic welcome when I arrived home. Thanks to my brother Terry for helping with admin tasks as I crossed America. Thanks to all my family, my brother Ged included, for supporting me and keeping me company along the way through the magic of Skype - it meant I never felt truly alone. Thanks to my dear friend Ve for kickstarting this crazy idea in the first place by giving me Anne Mustoe's book - little did she know what she'd started! I owe a great debt of thanks to Peter Yoong for nursing me for a month through a debilitating illness in Malaysia. Without his help I may never have finished the journey. Thanks to Petya and Ivo in Bulgaria for looking after me so well when my bike was stolen, giving me a base from which to carry on. Thanks to Calvin of Ghyllside Cycles, Ambleside, UK for his invaluable advice on purchasing a replacement bike. A big thanks goes to the wonderful family in Iran who gave me an unforgettable time staying in their home. Thanks to Ray in Calcutta for showing me the city and helping me with flight arrangements. To the many people who gave me free accommodation along the way, I thank you all - Ivana, Kathy and Sevket, Dawn, Beth and Rebecca, David and Hannah, Roger and Joanne, Mary-Lou and Richard and Rachelle and Flavio. Thanks to the people who fed me along the way and helped me with directions, and to my CrazyGuyonaBike readers who kept me going in the dark times. Thanks to Cath Bruzzone of b small Publishing for listening to my story and putting me in touch with Liz Nuttall of Handstand Press, and thanks to Liz for her invaluable advice which helped to finally get my manuscript in print. Thanks to Russell Holden of Pixeltweaks for his design work and to his wife Sharon for her editing. Thanks to Peter Langley for his brilliantly witty artwork and for his patience. My thanks go to Paul Loftus for taking the time to read the draft and for his kind words at the start of this book. Thanks to Neil Gunton who who does such a cracking job of hosting the CrazyGuyOnaBike website www. crazyguyonabike.com. And lastly, thanks to my friend Gill for the first full English on my return.

The Author

Ann Wilson was born in Barrow in Furness in 1950, the middle child of five and the only girl. She attended Our Lady's Secondary School for girls in Barrow and later studied Science with the Open University. Cycling did not figure prominently in her life until her mid-50s when she completed a ride from Carlisle to Ipswich. This turned out to be the precursor to her round-the-world cycling trip and a lasting love of cycle touring. Since that first long journey she has cycled from Canada to Mexico along the Pacific Coast, Morocco to Paris, Munich to Tblisi, Talinn to Amsterdam and from Houston Texas to the Atlantic and along the coast of Montenegro to Albania Ann has two children, a daughter who lives in her home town of Ulverston and a son who teaches in Japan. Before retiring she worked in the telecommunications industry.

Lightning Source UK Ltd.
Milton Keynes UK
UKHW04f1347150818
327278UK00001B/6/P